The UK Air Fryer

Cookbook for Beginners

365 Days Easy and Flavourful Air Fryer Recipes for Beginners and Busy People to Bake, Fry, Roast Meals Everyday

By Jasmine Rowley

Legal & Disclaimer

The content and information in this book is consistent and truthful, and it has been provided for informational, educational and business purposes only.

The illustrations in the book are from the website shutterstock.com, depositphoto.com and freepik. com and have been authorized.

The content and information contained in this book has been compiled from reliable sources, which are accurate based on the knowledge, belief, expertise and information of the Author. The author cannot be held liable for any omissions and/or errors.

Table of Content

INTRODUCTION

When the air fryer first came out, I was a little bit skeptical about whether it was able to hold up to all of the hype. It sounded pretty awesome, but I worried that it would be another overpriced appliance that would just sit on my kitchen counter and never get used. Boy was I wrong!

With this tool by my side, I was able to create some of the best meals around. From breakfast to lunch, dinner, and dessert, I pull out my air fryer at least a few times a week to create meals for the whole family. And now that I have accumulated a ton of recipes and worked through all of the flops, I want to share some of the best air fryer recipes with others who are looking to use their air fryers as well.

In this guidebook, we will go through a lot of great recipes that you are able to use when it comes to the air fryer, ensuring that you will be able to get some tasty treats, whether you have just purchased an air fryer for the first time or you have been a lifelong fan of this appliance and just want to try something new.

Worried about what a recipe will look like and want to make your decisions quick? I have included pictures with the recipes, in colour, to make sure that you can get a good idea of whether this is the perfect dish for you to make.

No matter how much you have used the air fryer in the past or how you plan to use it in the future, having some good recipes on hand for every meal can help make the air fryer worth every penny. Come take a look at some of these fantastic recipes and see which one is right for you.

CHAPTER 1: UNDERSTANDING THE BASICS OF THE AIR FRYER

In this guidebook, we are going to take some time to explore the tasty recipes that you are able to choose when you bring home an air fryer to use in your own kitchen. This is a great option for any kitchen because there is just so much that you are able to do with it. But before you jump in, let's take a moment to learn a bit more about the air fryer and why this is such a great kitchen appliance.

Why Use an Air Fryer?

There are a lot of reasons to choose to work with an air fryer. One of the primary benefits is that you can cook crispy and delicious foods without all of the oil. This will cut down on the amount of calories and fat compared to traditional deep frying.

The air fryer is also a good option to provide you with some of the crispy results that you want on all of your favorite foods. An air fryer is going to provide consistently crispy results, without you having to coat all of the ingredients in batter or immerse them in oil. It is all the great taste and crunch, without all of the bad stuff.

The speed is another benefit that customers can enjoy when they use an air fryer. You will find that after pushing the preheat function on the air fryer, you will be able to get the food done in just a few minutes, including some dishes that could traditionally take hours to get done with other appliances.

The right air fryer can also work as multiple appliance at once. There are several functions found in the air fryer for you to choose. You can use this not only as an air fryer but also an oven, and a dehydrator to name a few. This can help save space in your kitchen while giving you a lot of delicious meals that you can enjoy.

How the Air Fryer Works?

An air fryer is a useful kitchen appliance that will speed up the time it takes to create some of the tasty meals that your family needs, often in a fraction of the time of using other methods. But how does this unique tool work for you?

An air fryer is able to quickly circulate hot air throughout the inside. This is similar to what we see with a convection oven. This means that the fan that is inside of the device is going to make sure that all the hot air stuck inside will be able to go all over the food. In the end, you will have crispy food without all of the oil.

In this manner, all of the sides of the food will be exposed to the hot air, rather than just one part of it like with a traditional oven. This allows the food to become nice and crispy, without submerging it in the hot oils like traditional deep frying. If you want to have the taste and texture of deep frying, without all the unhealthy oils, and you want to cook meals quickly, then the air fryer is the best option.

The Main Functions of the Air Fryer

Many of the air fryers that you can choose will double as an oven as well. This allows you to have a number of different functions that you can enjoy when you turn the device on. In addition to air frying your food, you will be able to do a number of other tasks include:

* Baking: You will have to be careful about some of the baking you do because the hot air can be hard on some more delicate dishes. But it is possible to do some baking in your air fryer and they come out really good.

* Roasting: Roast everything to perfection in your air fryer. While a few recipes will ask that you add oil to help, it will still be a fraction of the oil that you need for deep frying. You get the great taste of roasting and deep fat frying, without all the additional calories those cooking methods entail.

* Dehydrating: If you would like to dehydrate some meats or other foods, you will find that this is the function that you will want to work with. You can add in the food, set the air fryer to a lower temperature, and then allow the food to cook for as long as you need.

* Keep warm: If you are not quite ready to serve that big meal to your family, then it is time to push the keep warm button. This will slow down some of the pressure and heat, while ensuring that everything will be ready when you need it.

* Preheat: It is a good idea to preheat the air fryer before you put any food inside. This allows it to get nice and warm and you will be able to add the food in and speed up some of the cooking time as well.

With all of the functions that are present on the air fryer, you will be able to make a lot of delicious meals, without having to worry about whether you have the right appliance around your home. This makes it the perfect option for you to enjoy for so many meals, as we will discuss in the following chapters.

How to Choose an Air Fryer

There are a few factors that you should consider when choosing an air fryer to help you make some tasty and delicious meals. You need to consider things like:

* The size of your family: A single person can get a lot of use out of the standard air fryer size, but you may need to go with a super-size model for your family or even consider the combination toaster oven to add to your kitchen.

* Basket style: You can consider the basket style when choosing the air fryer as well. The round basket is popular, but this one is more likely to require you to do batches to get the meal done. It is often best to choose a basket that is rectangular or square instead.

* The cost: Compare the cost of the different air fryers to help you find a good one. It is generally a bad idea to choose the cheapest air fryer on the market because it is usually priced so low for a reason. Consider researching all the options and finding a good combination of price versus the features you get.

* Look at the features: This doesn't mean you should pick out an air fryer just based on the features or how many features are present. You may not use all of them. Instead, consider which features are the most important to you and then make a purchase based on that.

* Brand: You may also want to look at the brand of air fryer to see if one is better for you than the others. There are so many brands out there that you can choose from, but read through reviews and find the one that is right for you.

The air fryer is a wonderful tool that can help you create a lot of delicious meals all in one. When you have your air fryer home and ready to go, take a look at some of the great recipes below to get the most value out of this amazing kitchen appliance.

BASIC KITCHEN CONVERSIONS & EQUIVALENTS

DRY MEASUREMENTS CONVERSION CHART

3 teaspoons = 1 tablespoon = 1/16 cup
6 teaspoons = 2 tablespoons = 1/8 cup
12 teaspoons = 4 tablespoons = ¼ cup
24 teaspoons = 8 tablespoons = ½ cup
36 teaspoons = 12 tablespoons = ¾ cup
48 teaspoons = 16 tablespoons = 1 cup

METRIC TO US COOKING CONVERSIONS

OVEN TEMPERATURES

120 °C = 250 °F
160 °C = 320 °F
180 °C = 350 °F
205 °C = 400 °F
220 °C = 425 °F

LIQUID MEASUREMENTS CONVERSION CHART

8 fluid ounces = 1 cup = ½ pint = ¼ quart
16 fluid ounces = 2 cups = 1 pint = ½ quart
32 fluid ounces = 4 cups = 2 pints = 1 quart = ¼ gallon
128 fluid ounces = 16 cups = 8 pints = 4 quarts = 1 gallon

BAKING IN GRAMS

1 cup flour = 140 grams
1 cup sugar = 150 grams
1 cup powdered sugar = 160 grams
1 cup heavy cream = 235 grams

VOLUME

1 milliliter = 1/5 teaspoon
5 ml = 1 teaspoon
15 ml = 1 tablespoon
240 ml = 1 cup or 8 fluid ounces
1 liter = 34 fluid ounces

WEIGHT

1 gram = .035 ounces
100 grams = 3.5 ounces
500 grams = 1.1 pounds
1 kilogram = 35 ounces

US TO METRIC COOKING CONVERSIONS

1/5 tsp = 1 ml
1 tsp = 5 ml
1 tbsp = 15 ml
1 fluid ounces = 30 ml
1 cup = 237 ml
1 pint (2 cups) = 473 ml
1 quart (4 cups) = .95 liter
1 gallon (16 cups) = 3.8 liters
1 oz = 28 grams
1 pound = 454 grams

BUTTER

1 cup butter = 2 sticks = 8 ounces = 230 grams = 16 tablespoons

WHAT DOES 1 CUP EQUAL

1 cup = 8 fluid ounces
1 cup = 16 tablespoons
1 cup = 48 teaspoons
1 cup = ½ pint
1 cup = ¼ quart
1 cup = 1/16 gallon
1 cup = 240 ml

BAKING PAN CONVERSIONS

9-inch round cake pan = 12 cups
10-inch tube pan =16 cups
10-inch bundt pan = 12 cups
9-inch springform pan = 10 cups
9 x 5 inch loaf pan = 8 cups
inch square pan = 8 cups

BAKING PAN CONVERSIONS

1 cup all-purpose flour = 4.5 oz
1 cup rolled oats = 3 oz
1 large egg = 1.7 oz
1 cup butter = 8 oz
1 cup milk = 8 oz
1 cup heavy cream = 8.4 oz
1 cup granulated sugar = 7.1 oz
1 cup packed brown sugar = 7.75 oz
1 cup vegetable oil = 7.7 oz
1 cup unsifted powdered sugar = 4.4 oz

CHAPTER 2: BREAKFAST

Omelette

Prep time: 5 minutes, Cook time: 8-10 minutes, Serves: 1

Ingredients:

3 eggs   2 tbsps. milk

Salt and pepper, to taste

30 g diced veggies (such as peppers, onions, and mushrooms)

25 g shredded cheese

Preparation Instructions:

1. Preheat your air fryer to 180°C.

2. In a small bowl, beat together the eggs, milk, salt, and pepper. Add the veggies and cheese to the bowl and mix well.

3. Pour the mixture into a small cake tin and put it in the air fryer basket and bake for 8-10 minutes, or until the omelette is cooked through and the edges are crispy.

Breakfast Burrito

Prep time: 5 minutes, Cook time: 5-7 minutes, Serves: 2

Ingredients:

cooking spray   4 small flour tortillas

100 g scrambled eggs

60 g black beans, drained and rinsed

75 g diced tomato   60 g diced avocado

25 g shredded cheese

Hot sauce, optional

Preparation Instructions:

1. Preheat your air fryer to 180°C and spritz the air fryer basket with cooking spray.

2. Lay out the tortillas on a flat surface.

3. Divide the eggs, black beans, tomato, avocado, and cheese evenly among the tortillas.

4. Roll the tortillas up tightly and place them seam-side down in the air fryer basket.

5. Air fry for 5-7 minutes until the burritos are heated through and the edges are crispy.

6. Serve with hot sauce, if desired.

French Toast

Prep time: 5 minutes, Cook time: 5-7 minutes, Serves: 2

Ingredients:

cooking spray   2 eggs   ½ tsp. cinnamon   4 slices bread
120 ml milk   1 tsp. vanilla extract   Butter, for spreading

Preparation Instructions:

1. Preheat your air fryer to 180°C and spritz the air fryer basket with cooking spray.

2. In a small bowl, whisk together the eggs, milk, vanilla extract, and cinnamon.

3. Dip each slice of bread into the egg mixture, making sure to coat both sides evenly.

4. Spread a thin layer of butter on one side of each slice of bread.

5. Place the bread in the air fryer basket, butter side down, and bake for 5-7 minutes, or until the French toast is golden brown.

Breakfast Energy Balls

Prep time: <5 minutes, Cook time: 5-7 minutes, Serves: 5

Ingredients:

80 g rolled oats 70 g almond butter

130 g honey   1 tsp. vanilla extract

35 g chocolate chips

25 g shredded coconut

Preparation Instructions:

1. In a medium bowl, mix together the oats, almond butter, honey, vanilla extract, chocolate chips, and coconut.

2. Roll the mixture into balls and place them in the air fryer basket.

3. Preheat your air fryer to 180°C and bake the balls for 5-7 minutes, or until heated through.

Tofu Scramble

Prep time: 15 minutes, Cook time: 10-12 minutes, Serves: 2

Ingredients:

cooking spray   2 tbsps. olive oil   mushrooms)
250 g tofu, drained and crumbled   1 tsp. turmeric   1 tsp. cumin
35 g diced veggies (such as peppers, onions, and   Salt and pepper, to taste

Preparation Instructions:

1. Preheat your air fryer to 180°C and spritz the air fryer basket with cooking spray.

2. In a small bowl, mix together the tofu, olive oil, veggies, turmeric, cumin, salt, and pepper.

3. Transfer the mixture to the air fryer basket and air fry for 10-12 minutes, or until the tofu is heated through and the edges are crispy.

Breakfast Quinoa

Prep time: 15 minutes, Cook time: 25 minutes, Serves: 2

Ingredients:

cooking spray   185 g quinoa

240 ml water   45 g diced ham

30 g diced veggies (such as peppers, onions, and mushrooms)

25 g shredded cheese

Preparation Instructions:

1. Preheat your air fryer to 180°C and spritz the air fryer basket with cooking spray.

2. In a small saucepan, bring the water to a boil.

3. Add the quinoa and stir.

4. Reduce the heat to low and simmer for 15 minutes, or until the quinoa is cooked.

5. Stir in the veggies, ham, and cheese.

6. Transfer the mixture to a cake tin and put the tin into the air fryer basket and bake for 5-7 minutes, or until heated through and the cheese is melted.

Banana Bread

Prep time: 15 minutes, Cook time: 30-35 minutes, Serves: 6-8

Ingredients:

125 g plain flour 1 tsp. baking powder

½ tsp. salt   60 g granulated sugar

60 g unsalted butter, melted

2 medium bananas, mashed (about 200 g)

1 large egg   1 tsp. vanilla extract

Preparation Instructions:

1. Preheat your air fryer to 180°C.

2. In a large mixing bowl, whisk together the flour, baking powder, and salt.

3. In a separate bowl, whisk together the sugar, melted butter, mashed bananas, egg, and vanilla extract.

4. Pour the wet ingredients into the dry ingredients and stir until just combined.

5. Pour the batter into a greased loaf pan that fits inside your air fryer.

6. Bake the banana bread in the preheated air fryer for 30-35 minutes, or until a toothpick inserted into the centre comes out clean.

7. Let the banana bread cool in the pan for a few minutes before removing and slicing.

Blueberry Muffins

Prep time: 15 minutes, Cook time: 12-15 minutes, Serves: 6-8

Ingredients:

120 g plain flour 1 tsp. baking powder

¼ tsp. salt   60 g granulated sugar

60 g unsalted butter, melted

120 ml milk   1 tsp. vanilla extract

120 g blueberries

Preparation Instructions:

1. Preheat your air fryer to 180°C.

2. In a large mixing bowl, whisk together the flour, baking powder, and salt.

3. In a separate bowl, whisk together the sugar, melted butter, milk, and vanilla extract.

4. Pour the wet ingredients into the dry ingredients and stir until just combined.

5. Gently fold in the blueberries.

6. Divide the muffin batter evenly among a muffin tin that fits inside your air fryer.

7. Bake the muffins in the preheated air fryer for 12-15 minutes, or until a toothpick inserted into the centre of a muffin comes out clean.

8. Let the muffins cool in the tin for a few minutes before removing and serving.

Sweet Potato Hash Browns

Prep time: 10 minutes, Cook time: 8-10 minutes, Serves: 4

Ingredients:

1 large sweet potato, peeled and grated

1 tbsp. plain flour   Salt, to taste

Pepper, to taste   Cooking spray

Preparation Instructions:

1. In a large bowl, mix together the grated sweet potato, flour, salt, and pepper.

2. Preheat your air fryer to 180°C.

3. Spray the air fryer basket with cooking spray. Scoop spoonfuls of the sweet potato mixture into the basket, flattening them into patties as you go.

4. Air fry the hash browns in the preheated air fryer for 8-10 minutes, or until they are crispy and golden brown on the outside.

5. Serve the hash browns hot.

Porridge Bread

Prep time: 1 hour 30 minutes, Cook time: 30-40 minutes, Serves: 8

Ingredients:

cooking spray   200 g rolled oats

350 ml water   5 g salt

3 g active dry yeast

25 g honey or maple syrup (optional, for sweetness)

Preparation Instructions:

1. In a medium-sized mixing bowl, combine the rolled oats, water, salt, and yeast. If you are using honey or maple syrup, add it now as well. Mix everything together until well combined.

2. Let the mixture sit at room temperature for at least 1 hour, or until it has doubled in size. The exact time will depend on the temperature and humidity in your kitchen, so you may need to adjust the time accordingly.

3. Preheat your air fryer to 190°C and spritz the air fryer basket with cooking spray.

4. Once the mixture has risen, use your hands to shape it into a loaf. You can either form it into a round shape or an oval shape, depending on your preference.

5. Place the loaf into the air fryer basket, making sure to leave enough space around it for the hot air to circulate.

6. Bake the bread for 30-40 minutes, or until it has formed a crust and sounds hollow when tapped on the bottom.

7. Remove the bread from the air fryer and allow it to cool for at least 15 minutes before slicing and serving.

8. The bread can be stored in a sealed container for up to 3 days at room temperature, or it can be frozen for later use.

Egg Cups

Prep time: 5 minutes, Cook time: 0 minutes, Serves: 4

Ingredients:

6 large eggs   Salt and pepper, to taste

30 g shredded cheese (cheddar, mozzarella, or a combination)

Optional fillings: diced vegetables, cooked bacon or sausage, chopped herbs or spring onions

Preparation Instructions:

1. Preheat your air fryer to 180°C.

2. Grease the cups of a muffin tin or use a silicone one.

3. Crack one egg into each muffin cup.

4. If desired, add in any fillings (vegetables, cooked meats, herbs) to each cup.

5. Sprinkle shredded cheese over the top of each egg.

6. Season the eggs with salt and pepper to taste.

7. Carefully place the muffin tin in the air fryer basket. Bake the eggs for 7-9 minutes, or until the whites are set and the yolks are cooked to your desired level of doneness.

8. Remove the muffin tin from the air fryer and let the eggs cool for a few minutes before removing them from the tin.

9. Serve the egg cups warm.

Granola

Prep time: 5 minutes, Cook time: 10-15 minutes, Serves: 6

Ingredients:

1.3 kg rolled oats   ½ tsp. salt

230 g chopped nuts (almonds, walnuts, pecans, etc.)

115 g shredded coconut

60 g maple syrup or honey

30 g oil (coconut, avocado, or vegetable oil)

5 ml vanilla extract

230 g dried fruit (raisins, cranberries, blueberries, etc.) (optional)

Preparation Instructions:

1. In a large bowl, mix together the oats, nuts, and coconut.

2. In a separate bowl, mix together the maple syrup or honey, oil, vanilla extract, and salt.

3. Pour the wet ingredients over the dry ingredients and stir until everything is evenly coated.

4. Spread the mixture evenly in the air fryer basket.

5. Bake at 150°C for 10-15 minutes, stirring every 5 minutes, or until the granola is golden brown and crispy.

6. If desired, add the dried fruit during the last minute of cooking to prevent burning.

7. Carefully remove the granola from the air fryer and let it cool completely before storing it in an airtight container.

Air Fryer Baked Oats

Prep time: 5 minutes, Cook time: 20-25 minutes, Serves: 5

Ingredients:

200 g rolled oats   500 ml milk

2 eggs 2 ripe bananas (mashed)

2 tbsps. honey or maple syrup

2 tsps. baking powder   1 tsp. vanilla extract

1 tsp. ground cinnamon

A pinch of salt

Optional: nuts, seeds, dried fruits, chocolate chips or any other desired toppings

Preparation Instructions:

1. In a mixing bowl, combine the oats, baking powder, cinnamon, and a pinch of salt.

2. In another bowl, mix together the eggs, milk, mashed banana, honey, and vanilla extract.

3. Add the wet ingredients to the dry ingredients and stir until well combined.

4. Pour the mixture into a greased air fryer safe dish that can fit in your air fryer basket.

5. Top with any desired toppings (nuts, seeds, dried fruits, chocolate chips etc.)

6. Bake at 180°C for 20-25 minutes or until golden brown and cooked through.

Breakfast Cookies

Prep time: 5 minutes, Cook time: 10-12 minutes, Serves: 6

Ingredients:

150 g rolled oats   50 g plain flour   2 tsps. baking powder   1 tsp. vanilla extract

1 ripe banana (mashed)   1 tsp. ground cinnamon A pinch of salt

2 tbsps. honey or maple syrup

Optional: nuts, seeds, dried fruits, chocolate chips or any other desired toppings

Preparation Instructions:

1. In a mixing bowl, combine the oats, flour, baking powder, cinnamon, and a pinch of salt.

2. In another bowl, mix together the mashed banana, honey, vanilla extract, and any desired toppings (nuts, seeds, dried fruits, chocolate chips etc.)

3. Add the wet ingredients to the dry ingredients and stir until well combined.

4. Use a cookie scoop or spoon to form the dough into balls, then flatten them slightly to form cookies.

5. Place the cookies in a greased and lined air fryer basket and bake at 180°C for around 10-12 minutes or until golden brown.

6. Carefully remove the cookies from the air fryer and let them cool on a wire rack before serving.

Breakfast Potatoes

Prep time: <5 minutes, Cook time: 20 minutes, Serves: 4

Ingredients:

cooking spray   2 tbsps. olive oil   1 tsp. paprika   1 tsp. garlic powder

500 g potatoes, peeled and diced into 1 cm cubes   Salt and pepper, to taste

Preparation Instructions:

1. Preheat your air fryer to 200°C and spritz the air fryer basket with cooking spray.

2. In a large bowl, mix together the potatoes, olive oil, paprika, garlic powder, salt, and pepper.

3. Place the mixture in the air fryer basket and air fry for 20-25 minutes, or until the potatoes are crispy and tender.

CHAPTER 3: FAMILY FAVOURITES

Fish and Chips

Prep time: 10 minutes, Cook time: 45 minutes, Serves: 4

Ingredients:

cooking spray   100 g flour
600 g fish fillets, cut into strips
Salt and pepper, to taste
Spices of your choice (paprika, garlic powder, cayenne pepper, etc.)
2 eggs, beaten 200 g breadcrumbs
800 g potatoes, cut into wedges

Preparation Instructions:

1. Preheat your air fryer to 180°C and spritz the air fryer basket with cooking spray.
2. Cut fish fillets into strips and season with salt, pepper, and your favourite spices.
3. Dip the fish in a mixture of flour and beaten egg, then coat with breadcrumbs.
4. Place the breaded fish in the air fryer basket.
5. Roast for around 10-12 minutes, or until golden brown and cooked through.
6. Peel and cut potatoes into wedges, season with salt, pepper, and your favourite spices.
7. Air fry at 180°C for around 20-25 minutes, or until crispy and golden brown.

Burgers

Prep time: 5 minutes, Cook time: 10-12 minutes, Serves: 4

Ingredients:

500 g beef mince	½ tsp. salt	Toppings of your choice (lettuce, tomato, cheese,
¼ tsp. black pepper	¼ tsp. garlic powder	ketchup, mustard, etc.)
¼ tsp. onion powder	4 buns	

Preparation Instructions:

1. In a mixing bowl, combine the beef mince, salt, pepper, garlic powder, and onion powder. Mix well.
2. Divide the mixture into 4 equal portions and shape each into a patty.
3. Preheat your air fryer to 200°C.
4. Place the patties in the air fryer basket and roast for 8-10 minutes, or until they reach an internal temperature of 71°C.
5. During the last minute of cooking, you can add cheese on top of each patty to melt it.
6. When the burgers are cooking, toast the buns in a toaster.
7. Assemble the burgers by placing a patty on the bottom half of each bun, and adding toppings as desired.
8. Serve immediately.

Meatballs

Prep time: 5 minutes, Cook time: 10-15 minutes, Serves: 4

Ingredients:

cooking spray   100 g breadcrumbs

500 g minced meat (beef, pork, turkey, or a mix)

50 g grated Parmesan cheese

2 cloves garlic, minced   1 egg

Preparation Instructions:

1. Preheat your air fryer to 180°C and spritz the air fryer basket with cooking spray.

2. Mix together minced meat, breadcrumbs, grated Parmesan cheese, minced garlic, and an egg.

3. Form into meatballs and place in the air fryer basket. Air fry at 180°C for around 10-15 minutes, or until cooked through.

Pork Chops

Prep time: <5 minutes, Cook time: 20 minutes, Serves: 4

Ingredients:

4 pork chops   Salt and pepper, to taste

Spices of your choice (paprika, garlic powder, cayenne pepper, etc.)

Preparation Instructions:

1. Preheat your air fryer to 180°C.

2. Season pork chops with salt, pepper, and your favourite spices.

3. Place the pork chops in the air fryer basket.

4. Roast for around 8-10 minutes per side, or until cooked through.

Stuffed Peppers

Prep time: 5 minutes, Cook time: 20-25 minutes, Serves: 4

Ingredients:

cooking spray   250 g cooked rice

4 bell peppers, halved and seeded

250 g minced meat

125 g diced tomatoes

50 g shredded cheese

Preparation Instructions:

1. Preheat your air fryer to 180°C and spritz the air fryer basket with cooking spray.

2. Cut bell peppers in half and remove the seeds.

3. Stuff them with a mixture of cooked rice, minced meat, diced tomatoes, and shredded cheese.

4. Place the stuffed peppers in the air fryer basket.

5. Air fry for around 20-25 minutes or until the peppers are tender and the filling is hot and bubbly.

BBQ Ribs

Prep time: <5 minutes, Cook time: 30 minutes, Serves: 4

Ingredients:

cooking spray   1 rack of pork or beef ribs
Your favourite BBQ rub or marinade

Preparation Instructions:

1. Preheat your air fryer to 180°C and spritz the air fryer basket with cooking spray.

2. Season a rack of pork or beef ribs with your favourite BBQ rub or marinade.

3. Place the rack in the air fryer basket.

4. Roast for around 25-30 minutes per side or until the meat is tender and falling off the bone.

Korean Style Beef

Prep time: 5 minutes, Cook time: 8-10 minutes, Serves: 4

Ingredients:

500 g beef sirloin, thinly sliced

2 tbsps. soy sauce 2 tbsps. brown sugar

2 cloves of garlic, minced

1 tbsp. sesame oil 1 tbsp. rice vinegar

½ tsp. red pepper flakes

Preparation Instructions:

1. In a mixing bowl, combine the beef, soy sauce, brown sugar, garlic, sesame oil, rice vinegar, and red pepper flakes. Mix well.

2. Preheat your air fryer to 180°C.

3. Place the beef in a single layer in the air fryer basket and roast for 8-10 minutes or until cooked through.

Asian Style Pork

Prep time: 5 minutes, Cook time: 8-10 minutes, Serves: 4-6

Ingredients:

500 g pork tenderloin, thinly sliced

3 cloves of garlic, minced   2 tbsps. soy sauce

2 tbsps. hoisin sauce   1 tbsp. rice vinegar

1 tbsp. honey   1 tsp. sesame oil

¼ tsp. black pepper

Preparation Instructions:

1. In a mixing bowl, combine the pork, garlic, soy sauce, hoisin sauce, rice vinegar, honey, sesame oil, and pepper. Mix well.

2. Preheat your air fryer to 180°C.

3. Place the pork in a single layer in the air fryer basket and air fry for 8-10 minutes or until cooked through.

Macaroni and Cheese Bites

Prep time: 5 minutes, Cook time: 10-12 minutes, Serves: 4

Ingredients:

cooking spray   100 g shredded cheese

200 g cooked macaroni pasta

55 g panko bread crumbs   2 eggs

Salt, pepper and any seasoning you like

Preparation Instructions:

1. Preheat your air fryer to 180°C and spritz the air fryer basket with cooking spray.

2. In a mixing bowl combine the macaroni, cheese, eggs, salt, pepper and any other seasoning you like.

3. Form the mixture into small balls.

4. Roll the balls in the panko bread crumbs.

5. Place the mac and cheese bites in the air fryer basket, making sure not to overcrowd it.

6. Bake for 10-12 minutes or until golden brown and crispy.

Lamb Kebabs

Prep time: 10 minutes, Cook time: 10-12 minutes, Serves: 4-6

Ingredients:

cooking spray   2 tbsps. olive oil

500 g lamb, cut into 2.5 cm cubes

2 cloves of garlic, minced

1 tsp. ground cumin   1 tsp. smoked paprika

½ tsp. salt   ¼ tsp. black pepper

1 red onion, cut into 2.5 cm chunks

1 red pepper, cut into 2.5 cm chunks

Skewers (if using wooden skewers, soak them in water for 30 minutes before using)

Preparation Instructions:

1. In a mixing bowl, combine the lamb cubes, garlic, cumin, smoked paprika, salt, pepper and olive oil. Mix well.

2. Thread the lamb cubes, onion, and bell pepper onto skewers.

3. Preheat your air fryer to 180°C and spritz the air fryer basket with cooking spray.

4. Place the skewers in the air fryer basket and roast for 10-12 minutes, turning occasionally, or until the lamb is cooked through and the vegetables are slightly charred.

5. Remove the skewers from the air fryer and let them rest for a few minutes before serving.

6. You can serve this delicious lamb kebabs with some yogurt based dips, or some herbs, or with pita bread.

Lamb Koftas

Prep time: 5-10 minutes, Cook time: 12-15 minutes, Serves: 4

Ingredients:

cooking spray   500 g lamb mince
1 onion, grated 2 cloves of garlic, minced

2 tsps. ground cumin   Salt and pepper, to taste
1 tbsp. chopped fresh mint and parsley

Preparation Instructions:

1. Preheat your air fryer to 180°C and spritz the air fryer basket with cooking spray.

2. In a mixing bowl, combine the lamb mince, onion, garlic, cumin, salt, pepper, mint, and parsley.

3. Mix well, then form the mixture into small sausage-shaped koftas.

4. Place the koftas in the air fryer basket, making sure not to overcrowd it.

5. Roast for 12-15 minutes or until the lamb is cooked through and golden brown.

Quesadillas

Prep time: 5 minutes, Cook time: 5 minutes, Serves: 2

Ingredients:

cooking spray   4 flour tortillas
100 g shredded cheese (cheddar, mozzarella, or your choice)

40 g diced cooked chicken or beef (optional)
35 g diced pepper, onions or any vegetables you like

Preparation Instructions:

1. Preheat your air fryer to 180°C and spritz the air fryer basket with cooking spray.

2. Place a tortilla on a plate and add the cheese, chicken or beef, bell pepper, and onions on half of the tortilla.

3. Fold the tortilla in half, pressing down gently to seal.

4. Place the quesadilla in the air fryer basket, making sure not to overcrowd it.

5. Air fry for 4-5 minutes on each side or until the tortilla is golden brown and the cheese is melted.

Pork and Apple Skewers

Prep time: 5-10 minutes, Cook time: 12-15 minutes, Serves: 4

Ingredients:

455 g pork loin, cut into 2.5 cm cubes
1 large Granny Smith apple, cut into 2.5 cm cubes

60 g Dijon mustard   2 tbsps. honey
1 tbsp. olive oil Salt and pepper, to taste

Preparation Instructions:

1. Preheat your air fryer to 180°C.

2. In a mixing bowl, combine the Dijon mustard, honey, olive oil, salt, and pepper.

3. Thread the pork and apple cubes onto skewers.

4. Brush the skewers with the mustard mixture.

5. Place the skewers in the air fryer basket, making sure not to overcrowd it.

6. Roast for 12-15 minutes or until the pork is cooked through and tender.

CHAPTER 4: FISH AND SEAFOOD

Crab Cakes

Prep time: 10 minutes, Cook time: 8-10 minutes, Serves: 4-6

Ingredients:

cooking spray   455 g crabmeat

120 g mayonnaise   50 g diced onion

40 g diced red pepper

2 cloves of garlic, minced

2 tbsps. Dijon mustard   1 tsp. paprika

30 g Panko breadcrumbs   1 egg

Salt and pepper, to taste

Preparation Instructions:

1. Preheat your air fryer to 180°C and spritz the air fryer basket with cooking spray.
2. In a mixing bowl, combine the crabmeat, mayonnaise, onion, red pepper, garlic, Dijon mustard, paprika, Panko, egg, salt and pepper.
3. Mix well, then form the mixture into cakes, about 8 cm in diameter.
4. Place the crab cakes in the air fryer basket, making sure not to overcrowd it.
5. Bake for 8-10 minutes or until golden brown and crispy.

Fish Fillets

Prep time: 5-10 minutes, Cook time: 8-10 minutes, Serves: 4

Ingredients:

4 white fish fillets (such as cod, tilapia, or halibut)
2 tbsps. lemon juice
2 cloves of garlic, minced
1 tsp. dried thyme   1 tbsp. olive oil
Salt and pepper, to taste

Preparation Instructions:

1. Preheat your air fryer to 180°C.
2. Mix the lemon juice, garlic, thyme, salt and pepper in a small bowl.
3. Place the fish fillets in the mixture and let them marinate for 10-15 minutes.
4. Remove the fish from the marinade and pat dry.
5. Brush the fish fillets with olive oil.
6. Place the fish fillets in the air fryer basket, making sure not to overcrowd it.
7. Bake for 8-10 minutes or until the fish flakes easily with a fork.

Air-fried Prawns

Prep time: 5 minutes, Cook time: 8-10 minutes, Serves: 4

Ingredients:

cooking spray   2 cloves of garlic, minced

455 g large prawns, peeled and deveined

2 tbsps. olive oil   Salt and pepper, to taste

1 tsp. paprika   1 tsp. dried oregano

Preparation Instructions:

1. Preheat your air fryer to 180°C and spritz the air fryer basket with cooking spray.
2. In a mixing bowl, combine the shrimp, garlic, olive oil, salt, pepper, paprika, and oregano.
3. Toss to coat the prawns evenly.
4. Place the prawns in the air fryer basket, making sure not to overcrowd it.
5. Air fry for 8-10 minutes or until pink and cooked through.

Lemon Garlic Salmon

Prep time: 5-10 minutes, Cook time: 8-10 minutes, Serves: 4

Ingredients:

4 salmon fillets 2 tbsps. olive oil

2 cloves of garlic, minced

¼ cup lemon juice   1 tsp. dried oregano

¼ tsp. salt   ¼ tsp. black pepper

Preparation Instructions:

1. Preheat your air fryer to 180°C.
2. In a mixing bowl, combine the olive oil, garlic, lemon juice, oregano, salt, and pepper.
3. Place the salmon fillets in the mixture and coat well.
4. Put the salmon in the air fryer basket and air fry for 8-10 minutes, or until the fish is cooked through and the internal temperature reaches 65°C.

Air-fried Scampi

Prep time: 5 minutes, Cook time: 8-10 minutes, Serves: 4-6

Ingredients:

455 g scampi (or large prawns), peeled and deveined   1 tsp. paprika   ½ tsp. salt

2 tbsps. olive oil 1 tsp. garlic powder   ¼ tsp. black pepper

Preparation Instructions:

1. In a bowl, combine the scampi, olive oil, garlic powder, paprika, salt, and pepper. Toss to coat the scampi evenly.
2. Place the scampi in the air fryer basket in a single layer.
3. Set the air fryer to 200°C and air fry the scampi for 8-10 minutes, or until they are pink and cooked through.
4. Serve the scampi hot with your favourite dipping sauce.

Scallops

Prep time: 5 minutes, Cook time: 8-10 minutes, Serves: 4,

Ingredients:

455 g sea scallops   2 tbsps. olive oil
1 tsp. garlic powder   1 tsp. dried parsley
½ tsp. salt   ¼ tsp. black pepper

Preparation Instructions:

1. In a small bowl, combine the olive oil, garlic powder, parsley, salt, and pepper.
2. Place the scallops in a shallow dish and brush the olive oil mixture onto both sides of the scallops.
3. Place the scallops in the air fryer basket in a single layer.
4. Set the air fryer to 180°C and air fry the scallops for 8-10 minutes, or until they are cooked through and slightly browned.
5. Serve the scallops hot with your favourite side dish or dipping sauce.

Mussels

Prep time: 15 minutes, Cook time: 3-5 minutes, Serves: 4

Ingredients:

900 g mussels, scrubbed and debearded
2 tbsps. butter   2 cloves garlic, minced
60 ml white wine   60 ml chicken stock
60 g cream
2 tbsps. chopped fresh parsley
¼ tsp. salt ¼ tsp. black pepper

Preparation Instructions:

1. In a large frying pan, melt the butter over medium heat. Add the garlic and cook for 1-2 minutes, or until fragrant.
2. Add the mussels, white wine, chicken stock, cream, parsley, salt, and pepper. Stir to combine.
3. Bring the mixture to a boil, then reduce the heat to low and simmer for 5-7 minutes, or until the mussels are cooked through and open. Discard any mussels that do not open.
4. Using a slotted spoon, transfer the mussels to the air fryer basket.
5. Set the air fryer to 180°C and air fry the mussels for 3-5 minutes, or until they are hot and the sauce is bubbly.
6. Serve the mussels hot with the sauce and bread to mop up the sauce.

Calamari

Prep time: 10 minutes, Cook time: 8-10 minutes, Serves: 4

Ingredients:

455 g cleaned squid, cut into rings ¼ tsp. black pepper 1 large egg
60 g flour 1 tsp. paprika 50 g breadcrumbs
1 tsp. garlic powder ½ tsp. salt

Preparation Instructions:

1. In a shallow dish, combine the flour, paprika, garlic powder, salt, and pepper.
2. In another shallow dish, beat the egg.
3. Place the breadcrumbs in a third shallow dish.
4. Dredge each squid ring in the flour mixture, shaking off any excess. Dip the rings into the beaten egg, then coat them with the breadcrumbs, pressing the breadcrumbs onto the rings to adhere.
5. Place the breaded squid rings in the air fryer basket.
6. Set the air fryer to 180°C and air fry the squid for 8-10 minutes, or until the squid is cooked through and the breadcrumbs are golden brown.
7. Serve the calamari hot with your favourite dipping sauce.

Cajun Cod

Prep time: 5 minutes, Cook time: 8-10 minutes, Serves: 4

Ingredients:

4 (100 g) cod fillets 2 tbsps. olive oil 1 tsp. dried oregano 1 tsp. dried thyme
2 tbsps. Cajun seasoning ¼ tsp. black pepper

Preparation Instructions:

1. In a small bowl, combine the olive oil, Cajun seasoning, oregano, thyme, and pepper.
2. Place the cod fillets in a shallow dish and brush the Cajun mixture onto both sides of the fillets.
3. Place the cod in the air fryer basket in a single layer.
4. Set the air fryer to 180°C and air fry the cod for 8-10 minutes, or until the cod is cooked through and flaky.

Teriyaki Salmon

Prep time: 5 minutes, Cook time: 8-10 minutes, Serves: 4

Ingredients:

4 (100 g) salmon fillets   60 g teriyaki sauce   1 tsp. sesame oil   1 tsp. grated ginger

2 tbsps. honey   1 tbsp. rice vinegar   1 clove garlic, minced

Preparation Instructions:

1. In a small bowl, combine the teriyaki sauce, honey, rice vinegar, sesame oil, ginger, and garlic.

2. Place the salmon fillets in a shallow dish and brush the teriyaki mixture onto both sides of the fillets.

3. Place the salmon in the air fryer basket in a single layer.

4. Set the air fryer to 180°C and bake the salmon for 8-10 minutes, or until the salmon is cooked through and the skin is crispy.

5. Serve the salmon hot with your favourite side dish.

Maple Mustard Salmon

Prep time: 5 minutes, Cook time: 8-10 minutes, Serves: 4

Ingredients:

cooking spray   4 (100 g) salmon fillets   1 tsp. dried thyme   ½ tsp. salt

2 tbsps. Dijon mustard   2 tbsps. maple syrup   ¼ tsp. black pepper

Preparation Instructions:

1. Preheat your air fryer to 180°C and spritz the air fryer basket with cooking spray.

2. In a small bowl, combine the Dijon mustard, maple syrup, thyme, salt, and pepper.

3. Place the salmon fillets in a shallow dish and brush the maple-mustard mixture onto both sides of the fillets.

4. Place the salmon in the air fryer basket in a single layer.

5. Bake for 8-10 minutes, or until the salmon is cooked through and the skin is crispy.

6. Serve the salmon hot with your favourite side dish.

Lemon Pepper Cod

Prep time: 5 minutes, Cook time: 8-10 minutes, Serves: 4

Ingredients:

4 (100 g) cod fillets   2 tbsps. olive oil   1 tsp. lemon pepper seasoning

2 tbsps. lemon juice   ½ tsp. salt   ¼ tsp. black pepper

Preparation Instructions:

1. In a small bowl, combine the olive oil, lemon juice, lemon pepper seasoning, salt, and pepper.

2. Place the cod fillets in a shallow dish and brush the lemon pepper mixture onto both sides of the fillets.

3. Place the cod in the air fryer basket in a single layer.

4. Set the air fryer to 180°C and air fry the cod for 8-10 minutes, or until the cod is cooked through and flaky.

Fish Pie

Prep time: 30 minutes, Cook time: 15-20 minutes, Serves: 4-6

Ingredients:

2 large potatoes, peeled and diced   2 cloves of garlic, minced

1 onion, diced   100 g frozen peas   2 tbsps. butter   2 tbsps. flour

100 g frozen corn   240 g cream   1 tsp. dried thyme   Salt and pepper, to taste

455 g white fish fillets, cut into bite-sized pieces   100 g grated cheddar cheese

Preparation Instructions:

1. Preheat your air fryer to 180°C.

2. In a pot of boiling water, cook the potatoes until they are tender. Drain and set aside.

3. In a pan, sauté the onion, garlic, and thyme in butter until the onion is translucent.

4. Stir in the flour and cook for 1 minute.

5. Gradually add the cream, stirring constantly, until the mixture thickens.

6. Stir in the fish, peas, corn, and cooked potatoes.

7. Season with salt and pepper, to taste.

8. Transfer the mixture to a greased oven-safe dish that will fit in your air fryer.

9. Top with grated cheese.

10. Place the dish in the air fryer basket and bake for 15-20 minutes, or until the cheese is melted and bubbly.

Fish Fingers

Prep time: 5 minutes, Cook time: 8-10 minutes, Serves: 4-6

Ingredients:

cooking spray
500 g white fish fillets, cut into finger-sized pieces

125 g plain flour	1 tsp. paprika
1 tsp. garlic powder	½ tsp. salt
¼ tsp. black pepper	2 eggs, beaten

125 g breadcrumbs
30 g grated Parmesan cheese

Preparation Instructions:

1. Preheat your air fryer to 180°C and spritz the air fryer basket with cooking spray.

2. In a shallow dish, combine the flour, paprika, garlic powder, salt, and pepper.

3. In a separate shallow dish, beat the eggs.

4. In another shallow dish, mix together the breadcrumbs and grated Parmesan cheese.

5. Dip each fish finger in the flour mixture, then the beaten eggs, and finally the breadcrumb mixture, pressing the breadcrumbs onto the fish to adhere.

6. Place the fish fingers in the air fryer basket, making sure they are not overcrowded.

7. Air fry the fish fingers for 8-10 minutes or until golden brown and cooked through.

Air Fryer Mackerel

Prep time: 5 minutes, Cook time: 8-10 minutes, Serves: 4

Ingredients:

4 mackerel fillets	2 tbsps. olive oil	2 tsps. dried oregano	1 tsp. paprika
2 cloves of garlic, minced		Salt and pepper, to taste	

Preparation Instructions:

1. Preheat your air fryer to 180°C.

2. In a small bowl, mix together the olive oil, garlic, oregano, paprika, salt and pepper.

3. Place the mackerel in a shallow dish and brush the seasoning mixture on both sides of the fish.

4. Place the fish in the air fryer basket, making sure they are not overcrowded.

5. Roast for 8-10 minutes or until cooked through and the skin is crispy.

CHAPTER 5: POULTRY

Lemon Herbed Chicken

Prep time: 30 + minutes, Cook time: 15-20 minutes, Serves: 4

Ingredients:

4 boneless, skinless chicken breasts (about 600g)
2 tbsps. olive oil 2 cloves of garlic, minced
1 tbsp. fresh lemon zest
1 tbsp. fresh thyme leaves
1 tsp. salt   ½ tsp. black pepper

Preparation Instructions:

1. In a small bowl, mix together the olive oil, garlic, lemon zest, thyme, salt, and pepper.
2. Place the chicken breasts in a large resealable plastic bag or a shallow dish.
3. Pour the marinade over the chicken, making sure that each breast is coated evenly. Marinate for at least 30 minutes or up to 2 hours in the refrigerator.
4. Preheat the air fryer to 180°C.
5. Place the chicken breasts in the air fryer basket, making sure they are not touching.
6. Roast the chicken for 15-20 minutes, or until the internal temperature reaches 74°C.

Kung Pao Chicken

Prep time: 5 minutes, Cook time: 8-10 minutes, Serves: 4

Ingredients:

cooking spray
500 g boneless, skinless chicken thighs, diced
2 tbsps. cornflour   2 tbsps. soy sauce
1 tbsp. rice vinegar   2 tsps. sugar

1 tsp. sesame oil   2 cloves of garlic, minced
1 tsp. grated ginger   2 tbsps. vegetable oil
¼ tsp. red pepper flakes
1 red pepper, diced   30 g unsalted peanuts

Preparation Instructions:

1. In a mixing bowl, combine the chicken, cornflour, soy sauce, rice vinegar, sugar, sesame oil, garlic, ginger, and red pepper flakes. Mix well.
2. Preheat your air fryer to 180°C and spritz the air fryer basket with cooking spray.
3. Place the chicken in a single layer in the air fryer basket and roast for 8-10 minutes or until cooked through.

Crispy Chicken Tenders

Prep time: 10 minutes, Cook time: 12-15 minutes, Serves: 4-6

Ingredients:

cooking spray   800 g chicken tenders
125 g flour   2 tsps. paprika
1 tsp. garlic powder   1 tsp. salt
½ tsp. black pepper   2 eggs
110 g panko breadcrumbs

Preparation Instructions:

1. In a shallow dish, mix together the flour, paprika, garlic powder, salt, and pepper.
2. In a separate shallow dish, beat the eggs.
3. Place the panko breadcrumbs in a third shallow dish.
4. Dip each chicken tender in the flour mixture, then the eggs, then the breadcrumbs, making sure that each tender is coated evenly.
5. Preheat your air fryer to 180°C and spritz the air fryer basket with cooking spray.
6. Place the chicken tenders in the air fryer basket, making sure they are not touching.
7. Roast for 12-15 minutes, or until the internal temperature reaches 74°C and the breading is golden brown and crispy.

Chicken Kiev

Prep time: 10 minutes, Cook time: 20-25 minutes, Serves: 4

Ingredients:

4 chicken breasts   4 cloves of garlic, minced   125 g flour   2 eggs, beaten
4 tbsps. of butter, at room temperature   100 g breadcrumbs   Oil, for brushing
1 tsp. of dried parsley   Salt and pepper, to taste

Preparation Instructions:

1. Preheat the air fryer to 180°C.
2. In a small bowl, mix together the minced garlic, butter, dried parsley, salt and pepper.
3. Place the chicken breasts between two sheets of plastic wrap and pound them with a meat mallet until they are an even thickness.
4. Place a spoonful of the butter mixture on one end of each chicken breast and roll them up, tucking in the ends to seal the butter inside.
5. Place the flour, beaten eggs, and breadcrumbs in separate shallow bowls.
6. Dip each chicken breast in the flour, then the eggs, and finally the breadcrumbs, making sure they are well coated.
7. Brush the chicken with a little oil and place them in the air fryer basket.
8. Roast for 20-25 minutes, or until the chicken is cooked through and the breadcrumbs are golden brown.
9. Remove from the air fryer and let them rest for a few minutes before serving.

Maple Glazed Turkey

Prep time: 10 minutes, Cook time: 50-60 minutes, Serves: 6-8

Ingredients:

cooking spray 1 turkey breast (about 1 kg)
75 g maple syrup 2 tbsps. Dijon mustard
1 tsp. dried sage Salt and pepper, to taste

Preparation Instructions:

1. Preheat your air fryer to 180°C and spritz the air fryer basket with cooking spray.
2. Mix together the maple syrup, mustard, sage, salt, and pepper in a small bowl.
3. Place the turkey breast in the air fryer basket and brush the mixture over the turkey.
4. Roast for 20-25 minutes per 500 g, or until the internal temperature reaches 74°C.

BBQ Turkey Breast

Prep time: 10 minutes, Cook time: 50-60 minutes, Serves: 6-8

Ingredients:

cooking spray Salt and pepper, to taste 1 tsp. smoked paprika
1 turkey breast (about 1 kg) 1 tsp. garlic powder
60 g BBQ sauce 1 tbsp. brown sugar

Preparation Instructions:

1. Preheat your air fryer to 180°C and spritz the air fryer basket with cooking spray.
2. Mix together the BBQ sauce, brown sugar, paprika, garlic powder, salt, and pepper in a small bowl.
3. Place the turkey breast in the air fryer basket and brush the mixture over the turkey.
4. Roast for 20-25 minutes per 500 g, or until the internal temperature reaches 74°C.

Duck Breast

Prep time: <5 minutes, Cook time: 8-10 minutes, Serves: 2

Ingredients:

2 duck breasts Salt and pepper, to taste Oil, for brushing

Preparation Instructions:

1. Preheat the air fryer to 180°C.
2. Score the duck skin in a crosshatch pattern, being careful not to cut into the meat.
3. Season the duck breasts with salt and pepper on both sides.
4. Place the duck breasts, skin side down, in the air fryer basket.
5. Roast for 8-10 minutes, or until the skin is crispy and the meat is cooked to your desired level of doneness.
6. Remove from the air fryer and let them rest for a few minutes before slicing and serving.

Buttermilk Chicken

Prep time: 10 minutes, Cook time: 15-20 minutes, Serves: 4

Ingredients:

4 boneless chicken thighs

125 g flour   1 tsp. paprika

1 tsp. garlic powder   1 tsp. onion powder

Salt and pepper, to taste

240 ml buttermilk   Oil, for brushing

Preparation Instructions:

1. Preheat the air fryer to 180°C.

2. In a shallow dish, mix together the flour, paprika, garlic powder, onion powder, salt and pepper.

3. Place the buttermilk in a separate shallow dish.

4. Dip each chicken thigh in the buttermilk, then coat in the flour mixture, pressing the flour mixture onto the chicken to make sure it sticks.

5. Brush the chicken with a little oil and place them in the air fryer basket.

6. Roast for 15-20 minutes, or until the chicken is cooked through and the coating is golden brown.

7. Remove from the air fryer and let them rest for a few minutes before serving.

Parmesan Crusted Chicken

Prep time: 10 minutes, Cook time: 15-20 minutes, Serves: 4

Ingredients:

4 boneless chicken breasts

50 g grated Parmesan cheese

65 g flour   2 eggs, beaten

100 g breadcrumbs

Salt and pepper, to taste

Oil, for brushing

Preparation Instructions:

1. Preheat the air fryer to 180°C.

2. Place the grated Parmesan cheese, flour, beaten eggs, breadcrumbs, salt and pepper in separate shallow bowls.

3. Dip each chicken breast in the flour, then the eggs, and finally the breadcrumbs, pressing the breadcrumbs onto the chicken to make sure they stick.

4. Brush the chicken with a little oil and place them in the air fryer basket.

5. Roast for 15-20 minutes, or until the chicken is cooked through and the coating is golden brown.

6. Remove from the air fryer and let them rest for a few minutes before serving.

Duck Leg

Prep time: 10 minutes, Cook time: 30-40 minutes, Serves: 4

Ingredients:

4 duck legs   2 cloves of garlic, minced   Salt and pepper, to taste   Oil, for brushing
1 tsp. of dried thyme   1 tsp. of dried rosemary

Preparation Instructions:

1. Preheat the air fryer to 180°C.
2. In a small bowl, mix together the minced garlic, dried thyme, dried rosemary, salt and pepper.
3. Rub the mixture all over the duck legs, making sure to coat them evenly.
4. Brush the duck legs with a little oil and place them in the air fryer basket.
5. Roast for 30-40 minutes, or until the skin is crispy and the meat is cooked through.
6. Remove from the air fryer and let them rest for a few minutes before serving.

Tandoori Chicken

Prep time: 30 + minutes, Cook time: 15-20 minutes, Serves: 4

Ingredients:

4 boneless chicken breasts
480 g plain yogurt
2 tbsps. of tandoori masala
2 cloves of garlic, minced
Salt and pepper, to taste   Oil, for brushing

Preparation Instructions:

1. Preheat the air fryer to 180°C.
2. In a small bowl, mix together the yogurt, tandoori masala, minced garlic, salt, and pepper.
3. Place the chicken breasts in a large resealable bag and pour the tandoori yogurt mixture over them. Seal the bag and toss to coat the chicken. Marinate for at least 30 minutes or overnight in the refrigerator.
4. Brush the chicken with a little oil and place them in the air fryer basket.
5. Roast for 15-20 minutes, or until the chicken is cooked through and the coating is golden brown

Orange Glazed Duck

Prep time: 5-10 minutes, Cook time: 15 minutes, Serves: 2

Ingredients:

2 duck breasts   70 g orange marmalade   ½ tsp. of black pepper   Oil, for brushing
2 tbsps. of soy sauce   1 tbsp. of honey

Preparation Instructions:

1. Preheat the air fryer to 180°C.

2. In a small bowl, mix together the orange marmalade, soy sauce, honey and black pepper.

3. Score the duck skin in a crosshatch pattern, being careful not to cut into the meat.

4. Brush the duck breasts with a little oil and place them in the air fryer basket, skin side down.

5. Roast for 8-10 minutes or until the skin is crispy.

6. Brush the glaze over the duck breasts and roast for an additional 2-3 minutes or until the glaze is caramelized.

7. Remove from the air fryer and let them rest for a few minutes before slicing and serving.

Five Spiced Duck

Prep time: 5-10 minutes, Cook time: 8-10 minutes, Serves: 2

Ingredients:

2 duck breasts   1 tsp. of five-spice powder   1 clove of garlic, minced   Oil, for brushing
1 tbsp. of soy sauce   1 tbsp. of honey

Preparation Instructions:

1. Preheat the air fryer to 180°C.

2. In a small bowl, mix together the five-spice powder, soy sauce, honey, minced garlic and some oil.

3. Score the duck skin in a crosshatch pattern, being careful not to cut into the meat.

4. Rub the marinade all over the duck breasts, making sure to coat them evenly.

5. Place the duck breasts, skin side down, in the air fryer basket.

6. Roast for 8-10 minutes or until the skin is crispy and the meat is cooked to your desired level of doneness.

7. Remove from the air fryer and let them rest for a few minutes before slicing and serving.

Spicy Turkey

Prep time: 5-10 minutes, Cook time: 20-25 minutes, Serves: 4

Ingredients:

1 turkey breast, butterflied

2 tbsps. of olive oil   1 tsp. of chili powder

1 tsp. of cumin   1 tsp. of garlic powder

Salt and pepper, to taste

Preparation Instructions:

1. Preheat the air fryer to 180°C.
2. In a small bowl, mix together the olive oil, chili powder, cumin, garlic powder, salt, and pepper.
3. Rub the mixture all over the turkey breast, making sure to coat it evenly.
4. Place the turkey breast in the air fryer basket.
5. Roast for 20-25 minutes, or until the turkey is cooked through.
6. Remove from the air fryer and let it rest for a few minutes before slicing and serving.

Citrus and Herb Turkey Breast

Prep time: 5-10 minutes, Cook time: 20-25 minutes, Serves: 4

Ingredients:

1 turkey breast, butterflied   2 tbsps. of olive oil   1 tsp. of dried sage   zest of 1 orange

1 tsp. of dried thyme   1 tsp. of dried oregano   zest of 1 lemon Salt and pepper, to taste

Preparation Instructions:

1. Preheat the air fryer to 180°C.
2. In a small bowl, mix together the olive oil, dried thyme, dried oregano, dried sage, orange zest, lemon zest, salt, and pepper.
3. Rub the mixture all over the turkey breast, making sure to coat it evenly.
4. Place the turkey breast in the air fryer basket.
5. Roast for 20-25 minutes, or until the turkey is cooked through.
6. Remove from the air fryer and let it rest for a few minutes before slicing and serving.

CHAPTER 6: VEGETARIAN MAINS

Vegetable Kebabs

Prep time: 10 minutes, Cook time: 10 minutes, Serves: 4

Ingredients:

250 g mixed vegetables (such as peppers, onions, mushrooms, and cherry tomatoes), cut into bite-size pieces

2 tbsps. of olive oil   1 tsp. of dried oregano

1 tsp. of dried thyme   Salt and pepper, to taste

Preparation Instructions:

1. Preheat the air fryer to 180°C.

2. In a small bowl, mix together the olive oil, oregano, thyme, salt, and pepper.

3. Thread the vegetables onto skewers, alternating between different types of vegetables.

4. Brush the skewers with the olive oil mixture.

5. Place the skewers in the air fryer basket.

6. Roast for 8-10 minutes, or until the vegetables are tender and slightly charred, turning halfway through.

Tofu

Prep time: 30 + minutes, Cook time: 15-20 minutes, Serves: 4

Ingredients:

400 g extra-firm tofu, drained and pressed

2 tbsps. of soy sauce   2 tbsps. of hoisin sauce

2 cloves of garlic, minced

1 tsp. of grated ginger   1 tsp. of sesame oil

1 tbsp. of cornflour

Preparation Instructions:

1. Preheat the air fryer to 180°C.

2. In a small bowl, mix together the soy sauce, hoisin sauce, minced garlic, grated ginger, sesame oil, and cornflour.

3. Cut the tofu into cubes and place them in a large resealable bag. Pour the marinade over the tofu and toss to coat. Let it marinate for at least 30 minutes or overnight in the refrigerator.

4. Place the tofu cubes in the air fryer basket and air fry for 15-20 minutes, or until crispy and golden brown, turning halfway through.

5. Remove from the air fryer and serve with your favourite dipping sauce.

Asian Style Tofu Kebabs

Prep time: 30 + minutes, Cook time: 15-20 minutes, Serves: 4

Ingredients:

400 g extra-firm tofu, drained and pressed

2 tbsps. of soy sauce   2 tbsps. of hoisin sauce

2 cloves of garlic, minced

1 tsp. of grated ginger   1 tsp. of sesame oil

1 tbsp. of cornflour   Oil, for brushing

Salt and pepper, to taste

Preparation Instructions:

1. Preheat the air fryer to 180°C.
2. In a small bowl, mix together the soy sauce, hoisin sauce, minced garlic, grated ginger, sesame oil, cornflour, salt and pepper.
3. Cut the tofu into cubes and place them in a large resealable bag. Pour the marinade over the tofu and toss to coat. Let it marinate for at least 30 minutes or overnight in the refrigerator.
4. Thread the tofu cubes onto skewers.
5. Brush the skewers with a little oil and place them in the air fryer basket.
6. Roast for 15-20 minutes, or until crispy and golden brown, turning halfway through.
7. Remove from the air fryer and serve with your favourite dipping sauce.

Pakoras

Prep time: 10 minutes, Cook time: 8-10 minutes, Serves: 4

Ingredients:

250 g gram flour   Oil, for brushing

1 tsp. of cumin powder

1 tsp. of coriander powder

1 tsp. of ginger powder

½ tsp. of red chili powder

Salt, to taste   Water, as needed

250 g mixed vegetables (such as onions, peppers, carrots, and cauliflower), cut into small pieces

Preparation Instructions:

1. Preheat the air fryer to 180°C.
2. In a large mixing bowl, combine the gram flour, cumin powder, coriander powder, ginger powder, red chili powder and salt. Slowly add enough water to make a thick batter. The consistency should be thick enough to coat the vegetables.
3. Dip the vegetables into the batter, making sure they are well coated.
4. Place the battered vegetables in the air fryer basket and brush them with a little oil.
5. Air fry for 8-10 minutes or until golden brown and crispy.
6. Remove from the air fryer and drain on a paper towel.
7. Serve hot with your favourite dipping sauce.

Falafel

Prep time: 10 minutes, Cook time: 8-10 minutes, Serves: 4

Ingredients:

250 g dried chickpeas, soaked overnight and drained

1 onion, chopped   1 tsp. of cumin powder

2 cloves of garlic, minced

¼ cup of fresh parsley, chopped

¼ cup of fresh coriander, chopped

1 tsp. of coriander powder

Salt and pepper, to taste   Oil, for brushing

Preparation Instructions:

1. Preheat the air fryer to 180°C.
2. In a food processor, pulse together the soaked chickpeas, onion, garlic, parsley, coriander, cumin powder, coriander powder, salt and pepper until well combined and forms a paste.
3. Form the mixture into small balls or patties.
4. Brush the falafel with a little oil and place them in the air fryer basket.
5. Bake for 8-10 minutes or until golden brown and crispy.
6. Remove from the air fryer and drain on a paper towel.
7. Serve hot with your favourite dipping sauce.

Parmesan Aubergine

Prep time: 30 + minutes, Cook time: 20 minutes, Serves: 4

Ingredients:

cooking spray   240 g marinara sauce

2 aubergines, sliced into ½ cm rounds

Salt and pepper, to taste

125 g flour   2 eggs, beaten

100 g breadcrumbs

100 g grated Parmesan cheese

120 g shredded mozzarella cheese

Preparation Instructions:

1. Preheat your air fryer to 180°C and spritz the air fryer basket with cooking spray.
2. Place the aubergine slices on a baking sheet and sprinkle with salt and pepper. Allow to sit for 30 minutes to release excess moisture.
3. Place the flour in a shallow dish, the beaten eggs in a second dish, and the breadcrumbs in a third dish.
4. Dip the aubergine slices in flour, then eggs, and finally in breadcrumbs, pressing the breadcrumbs onto the aubergine to make sure they stick.
5. Place the breaded aubergine slices in the air fryer basket and air fry for 8-10 minutes or until golden brown.
6. Remove from the air fryer and drain on a paper towel.
7. In a baking dish, layer the cooked aubergine slices, marinara sauce, Parmesan cheese and mozzarella cheese.
8. Place the dish back in the air fryer and air fry for another 5-7 minutes or until the cheese is melted and bubbly.
9. Remove from the air fryer and let it sit for a few minutes before serving.

Cauliflower Buffalo Wings

Prep time: 5-10 minutes, Cook time: 25 minutes, Serves: 4

Ingredients:

cooking spray   ½ tsp. of onion powder

1 head of cauliflower, cut into florets

60 g flour   ½ tsp. of garlic powder

Salt and pepper, to taste

120 ml hot sauce   2 tbsps. of butter, melted

Blue cheese dressing, for dipping

Preparation Instructions:

1. Preheat your air fryer to 180°C and spritz the air fryer basket with cooking spray.

2. In a large mixing bowl, combine the flour, garlic powder, onion powder, salt, and pepper.

3. Dip the cauliflower florets in the flour mixture, making sure they are well coated.

4. Place the cauliflower florets in the air fryer basket and roast for 15-20 minutes or until tender and crispy.

5. Remove from the air fryer and toss in the hot sauce and melted butter.

6. Place the cauliflower florets back in the air fryer and roast for another 2-3 minutes.

7. Remove from the air fryer and serve with blue cheese dressing.

Veggie Fried Rice

Prep time: 10 minutes, Cook time: 10 minutes, Serves: 4

Ingredients:

2 tbsps. of oil   1 onion, diced

2 cloves of garlic, minced

400 g cooked rice

150 g mixed vegetables (such as peas, carrots,

corn, and peppers), diced

2 eggs, beaten 2 tbsps. of soy sauce

Salt and pepper, to taste

Preparation Instructions:

1. Preheat the air fryer to 180°C.

2. In a pan or wok, heat the oil and sauté the onion and garlic until softened.

3. Add the rice and vegetables and stir-fry for 2-3 minutes.

4. Push the rice mixture to the side of the pan and pour the beaten eggs in the centre. Scramble the eggs and then mix them with the rice mixture.

5. Stir in the soy sauce, salt and pepper.

6. Line the air fryer basket with some parchment paper.

7. Place the rice mixture in the air fryer basket and air fry for 8-10 minutes, or until heated through and crispy.

8. Remove from the air fryer and serve.

Cauliflower Steaks

Prep time: 5 minutes, Cook time: 15-20 minutes, Serves: 4

Ingredients:

1 head of cauliflower, cut into 2 cm steaks
2 tbsps. of olive oil   1 tsp. of cumin

1 tsp. of smoked paprika
Salt and pepper, to taste

Preparation Instructions:

1. Preheat the air fryer to 180°C.

2. In a small bowl, mix together the olive oil, cumin, smoked paprika, salt and pepper.

3. Brush the cauliflower steaks with the mixture and place them in the air fryer basket.

4. Roast for 15-20 minutes, or until tender and golden brown, turning halfway through.

5. Remove from the air fryer and serve as a main dish.

Portobello Mushrooms

Prep time: 5 minutes, Cook time: 8-10 minutes, Serves: 4

Ingredients:

cooking spray
4 large portobello mushrooms, stems removed

2 tbsps. of olive oil
1 tsp. of dried thyme

2 cloves of garlic, minced
Salt and pepper, to taste

Preparation Instructions:

1. Preheat your air fryer to 180°C and spritz the air fryer basket with cooking spray.

2. In a small bowl, mix together the olive oil, minced garlic, dried thyme, salt and pepper.

3. Brush the mixture over the portobello mushrooms, making sure to coat them evenly.

4. Place the mushrooms in the air fryer basket, gill side up.

5. Air fry for 8-10 minutes, or until tender and golden brown.

7. Remove from the air fryer and serve as a main dish.

Quinoa Stuffed Peppers

Prep time: 10 minutes, Cook time: 20 minutes, Serves: 4

Ingredients:

cooking spray   250 g cooked quinoa
4 peppers, halved lengthwise and seeded
250 g cooked black beans
1 red onion, diced   1 tsp. of cumin powder

2 cloves of garlic, minced
1 tsp. of smoked paprika
Salt and pepper, to taste
50 g shredded cheddar cheese

Preparation Instructions:

1. Preheat your air fryer to 180°C and spritz the air fryer basket with cooking spray.

2. In a mixing bowl, combine the cooked quinoa, black beans, onion, garlic, cumin, smoked paprika, salt, and pepper.

3. Stuff the pepper halves with the quinoa mixture and place them in the air fryer basket.

4. Air fry for 15-20 minutes or until the peppers are tender.

5. Remove from the air fryer, top with shredded cheese and air fry for another 2-3 minutes or until cheese is melted.

CHAPTER 7: VEGETARIAN VEGETABLES AND SIDES

Chickpea and Sweet Potato Fritters

Prep time: 10 minutes, Cook time: 10 minutes, Serves: 4

Ingredients:

1 can of chickpeas, drained and rinsed

1 sweet potato, peeled and grated

30 g flour   30 g polenta

1 tbsp. of cumin powder

1 tsp. of coriander powder

½ tsp. of baking powder

Salt and pepper, to taste

Oil, for brushing

Preparation Instructions:

1. Preheat the air fryer to 180°C.

2. In a food processor, pulse together the chickpeas, sweet potato, flour, polenta, cumin powder, coriander powder, baking powder, salt and pepper until a thick paste forms.

3. Form the mixture into small patties.

4. Brush the patties with a little oil and place them in the air fryer basket.

5. Bake for 8-10 minutes or until golden brown and crispy, flipping halfway through.

6. Remove from the air fryer and drain on a paper towel.

Roasted Cauliflower

Prep time: 5 minutes, Cook time: 10 minutes, Serves: 4-6

Ingredients:

400 g cauliflower florets

2 tbsps. of olive oil

1 tsp. of smoked paprika

Salt and pepper, to taste

Preparation Instructions:

1. Preheat the air fryer to 180°C.

2. In a large mixing bowl, toss the cauliflower florets with olive oil, smoked paprika, salt and pepper.

3. Place the cauliflower florets in the air fryer basket and roast for 8-10 minutes or until tender and crispy, flipping halfway through.

4. Remove from the air fryer and serve as a side dish or as a topping for salads or bowls.

Crispy Kale

Prep time: <5 minutes, Cook time: 5-8 minutes, Serves: 4

Ingredients:

1 bunch of kale, washed and dried   Salt and pepper, to taste

2 tbsps. of olive oil   1 tsp. of garlic powder

Preparation Instructions:

1. Preheat the air fryer to 180°C.

2. Remove the kale leaves from the thick stem, and tear into bite-size pieces.

3. In a large mixing bowl, toss the kale with olive oil, garlic powder, salt, and pepper.

4. Place the kale in the air fryer basket and air fry for 5-8 minutes or until crispy and slightly charred, flipping halfway through.

Sweet Potato Fries

Prep time: 5 minutes, Cook time: 10-15 minutes, Serves: 4-6

Ingredients:

600 g sweet potatoes, peeled and cut into fries

2 tbsps. of olive oil   1 tsp. of smoked paprika

Salt and pepper, to taste

Preparation Instructions:

1. Preheat the air fryer to 180°C.

2. In a large mixing bowl, toss the sweet potato fries with olive oil, smoked paprika, salt, and pepper.

3. Place the sweet potato fries in the air fryer basket and air fry for 10-15 minutes or until tender and crispy, flipping halfway through.

4. Remove from the air fryer and serve as a side dish.

Air Fryer Baked Courgette

Prep time: 5 minutes, Cook time: 8-10 minutes, Serves: 4-6

Ingredients:

2 courgettes, sliced   2 tbsps. of olive oil   1 tsp. of dried basil   Salt and pepper, to taste

Preparation Instructions:

1. Preheat the air fryer to 180°C.

2. In a large mixing bowl, toss the courgette slices with olive oil, dried basil, salt, and pepper.

3. Place the courgette slices in the air fryer basket and air fry for 8-10 minutes or until tender and slightly charred, flipping halfway through.

4. Remove from the air fryer and serve as a side dish or as a topping for salads or bowls.

Air Fryer Baked Butternut Squash

Prep time: 5 minutes, Cook time: 10-15 minutes, Serves: 4-6

Ingredients:

400 g butternut squash, peeled and diced
1 tbsp. of olive oil   Salt and pepper, to taste
1 tsp. of cinnamon powder

Preparation Instructions:

1.   Preheat the air fryer to 180°C.

2.   In a large mixing bowl, toss the butternut squash with olive oil, cinnamon powder, salt, and pepper.

3.   Place the butternut squash in the air fryer basket and bake for 10-15 minutes or until tender and slightly charred, flipping halfway through.

4.   Remove from the air fryer and serve as a side dish.

Garlic Parmesan Brussels Sprouts

Prep time: 5 minutes, Cook time: 10 minutes, Serves: 4-6

Ingredients:

400 g Brussels sprouts, trimmed and halved
2 tbsps. of olive oil   2 cloves of garlic, minced
2 tbsps. of grated Parmesan cheese
Salt and pepper, to taste

Preparation Instructions:

1. Preheat the air fryer to 180°C.
2. In a large mixing bowl, toss the Brussels sprouts with olive oil, minced garlic, grated Parmesan cheese, salt, and pepper.
3. Place the Brussels sprouts in the air fryer basket and air fry for 8-10 minutes or until tender and crispy, flipping halfway through.
4. Remove from the air fryer and serve as a side dish.

Air Fryer Roasted Beetroot

Prep time: 5 minutes, Cook time: 8-10 minutes, Serves: 4-6

Ingredients:

400 g beetroot, peeled and diced   Salt and pepper, to taste

2 tbsps. of olive oil   1 tsp. of dried rosemary

Preparation Instructions:

1. Preheat the air fryer to 180°C.
2. In a large mixing bowl, toss the beets with olive oil, dried rosemary, salt, and pepper.
3. Place the beets in the air fryer basket and roast for 8-10 minutes or until tender and slightly charred, flipping halfway through.
4. Remove from the air fryer and serve as a side dish.

Aubergine Fries

Prep time: 5 minutes, Cook time: 8-10 minutes, Serves: 4-6

Ingredients:

2 medium aubergines   100 g breadcrumbs   1 tsp. of dried thyme

60 g flour   2 large eggs, beaten   Salt and pepper, to taste   Oil, for brushing

Preparation Instructions:

1. Preheat the air fryer to 180°C.
2. Cut the aubergine into fries shape.
3. Place the flour, beaten eggs, and breadcrumbs in separate shallow dishes.
4. Mix thyme, salt and pepper in the breadcrumbs.
5. Dip the aubergine fries into the flour, then the beaten eggs, and finally the breadcrumbs mixture, pressing the breadcrumbs onto the aubergine to adhere.
6. Brush the aubergine, fries with a little oil and place them in the air fryer basket.
7. Air fry for 8-10 minutes or until golden brown and crispy, turning halfway through.

Air Fryer Roasted Vegetables

Prep time: 5 minutes, Cook time: 10-15 minutes, Serves: 4-6

Ingredients:

400 g vegetables of your choice (e.g. peppers, courgette, aubergine, onion, carrot, broccoli, cauliflower)

2 tbsps. olive oil

1 tsp. dried herbs of your choice (e.g. rosemary, thyme, oregano)

Salt and pepper, to taste

Preparation Instructions:

1. Preheat the air fryer to 180°C.
2. Cut the vegetables into bite-size pieces.
3. In a large mixing bowl, toss the vegetables with olive oil, dried herbs, salt, and pepper.
4. Place the vegetables in the air fryer basket and roast for 10-15 minutes or until tender and slightly charred, flipping halfway through.

Zesty Parmesan Asparagus

Prep time: <5 minutes, Cook time: 8-10 minutes, Serves: 4-6

Ingredients:

400 g asparagus, trimmed

2 tbsps. of olive oil   1 tsp. of lemon zest

1 tbsp. of lemon juice   Salt and pepper, to taste

2 tbsps. of grated Parmesan cheese

Preparation Instructions:

1. Preheat the air fryer to 180°C.
2. In a large mixing bowl, toss the asparagus with olive oil, lemon zest, lemon juice, grated Parmesan cheese, salt, and pepper.
3. Place the asparagus in the air fryer basket and air fry for 8-10 minutes or until tender and slightly charred, flipping halfway through.

Roasted Peppers

Prep time: <5 minutes, Cook time: 8-10 minutes, Serves: 4-6

Ingredients:

400 g peppers, seeded and sliced   Salt and pepper, to taste

2 tbsps. of olive oil   1 tsp. of smoked paprika

Preparation Instructions:

1. Preheat the air fryer to 180°C.
2. In a large mixing bowl, toss the peppers with olive oil, smoked paprika, salt, and pepper.
3. Place the bell peppers in the air fryer basket and roast for 8-10 minutes or until tender and slightly charred, flipping halfway through.

CHAPTER 8: PIZZAS, WRAPS AND SANDWICHES

Veggie Sandwich

Prep time: 5 minutes, Cook time: 3-5 minutes, Serves: 2

Ingredients:

cooking spray   4 slices of bread

100 g of sliced cucumber

100 g of sliced tomatoes

100 g of sliced onion

100 g of sliced mushrooms

100 g of sliced avocado

2 tbsps. of mayonnaise

Salt and pepper, to taste

Preparation Instructions:

1. Preheat your air fryer to 180°C and spritz the air fryer basket with cooking spray.

2. Spread mayonnaise on one side of each slice of bread.

3. Place the vegetables between two slices of bread and press the edges together to make a sandwich.

4. Place the sandwich in the air fryer basket and bake for 3-5 minutes or until the bread is golden brown and the vegetables are tender, flipping halfway through.

5. Remove from the air fryer and let it cool for a few minutes before serving.

6. You can also add any other fillings to your sandwich like cheese, hummus, or salsa for more flavour and texture.

BBQ Chicken Sandwich

Prep time: 5 minutes, Cook time: 3-5 minutes, Serves: 2

Ingredients:

cooking spray   4 slices of bread

200 g of cooked, shredded chicken

100 g of BBQ sauce   2 tbsps. of butter

100 g of grated cheddar cheese

Salt and pepper, to taste

Preparation Instructions:

1. Preheat your air fryer to 180°C and spritz the air fryer basket with cooking spray.

2. Spread butter on one side of each slice of bread.

3. In a mixing bowl, combine the shredded chicken, BBQ sauce, salt, and pepper. Mix until well combined.

4. Spread the BBQ chicken mixture on one slice of bread, top with grated cheese.

5. Place the sandwich in the air fryer basket and bake for 3-5 minutes or until the bread is golden brown and the cheese is melted, flipping halfway through.

Tuna Melt

Prep time: 5 minutes, Cook time: 3-5 minutes, Serves: 2

Ingredients:

cooking spray   Salt and pepper, to taste
200 g of canned tuna, drained

100 g of diced celery   100 g of diced onion
2 tbsps. of mayonnaise
100 g of grated cheddar cheese

Preparation Instructions:

1. Preheat your air fryer to 180°C and spritz the air fryer basket with cooking spray.
2. In a mixing bowl, combine the canned tuna, diced celery, onion, mayonnaise, salt, and pepper. Mix until well combined.
3. Spread the tuna mixture on one slice of bread, top with grated cheese.
4. Place the sandwich in the air fryer basket and bake for 3-5 minutes or until the bread is golden brown and the cheese is melted, flipping halfway through.

Greek Wrap

Prep time: <5 minutes, Cook time: 2-3 minutes, Serves: 4

Ingredients:

4 tortilla wraps   100 g of diced tomatoes
200 g of cooked and shredded lamb or chicken
100 g of diced cucumber

100 g of crumbled feta cheese
2 tbsps. of tzatziki sauce   2 tbsps. of olive oil
Salt and pepper, to taste

Preparation Instructions:

1. Preheat the air fryer to 180°C.
2. Place the cooked and shredded lamb or chicken in the centre of each tortilla wrap.
3. Top with diced tomatoes, cucumber, crumbled feta cheese, and tzatziki sauce.
4. Roll the tortilla wraps tightly and brush the tops with olive oil.
5. Place the wraps in the air fryer basket and air fry for 2-3 minutes or until the tortilla is golden brown and crispy.

BBQ Chicken Pizza

Prep time: <5 minutes, Cook time: 10 minutes, Serves: 2-4

Ingredients:

1 pre-made pizza base   100 g of BBQ sauce
100 g of shredded chicken

100 g of diced red onions
50 g of cheddar cheese

Preparation Instructions:

1. Preheat the air fryer to 180°C.
2. Place the pre-made pizza crust in the air fryer basket and bake for 2-3 minutes or until it starts to puff up and become slightly crispy.
3. Remove the crust from the air fryer and spread the BBQ sauce over the crust, leaving a small border around the edge.
4. Add shredded chicken, diced red onions and cheddar cheese on top of the BBQ sauce.
5. Place the pizza back in the air fryer basket and bake for an additional 5-7 minutes or until the cheese is melted and the crust is golden brown.

French Dip Sandwich

Prep time: 5 minutes, Cook time: 3-5 minutes, Serves: 2

Ingredients:

4 slices of bread   2 tbsps. of beef stock

100 g of thinly sliced roast beef

2 cloves of minced garlic   2 tbsps. of butter

Salt and pepper, to taste

Preparation Instructions:

1. Preheat the air fryer to 180°C.
2. Spread butter on one side of each slice of bread.
3. Place the roast beef between two slices of bread and press the edges together to make a sandwich.
4. Place the sandwich in the air fryer basket and bake for 3-5 minutes or until the bread is golden brown and the roast beef is heated through, flipping halfway through.
5. Remove from the air fryer and let it cool for a few minutes before serving.
6. Serve with the beef stock for dipping.

Cuban Sandwich

Prep time: 5 minutes, Cook time: 3-5 minutes, Serves: 2

Ingredients:

cooking spray   4 slices of bread   100 g of dill pickles, sliced

100 g of thinly sliced roast pork   2 tbsps. of yellow mustard

100 g of thinly sliced ham   2 tbsps. of butter

100 g of thinly sliced Swiss cheese   Salt and pepper, to taste

Preparation Instructions:

1. Preheat your air fryer to 180°C and spritz the air fryer basket with cooking spray.
2. Spread butter on one side of each slice of bread.
3. Spread mustard on one side of the bread.
4. Place the roast pork, ham, Swiss cheese, and pickles between two slices of bread and press the edges together to make a sandwich.
5. Place the sandwich in the air fryer basket and bake for 3-5 minutes or until the bread is golden brown and the cheese is melted, flipping halfway through.

Falafel Sandwich

Prep time: 5 minutes, Cook time: 3-5 minutes, Serves: 2

Ingredients:

cooking spray   Salt and pepper, to taste
4 slices of pita bread   200 g of falafel balls
100 g of hummus   100 g of diced tomatoes
100 g of diced cucumber
2 tbsps. of tahini   2 tbsps. of lemon juice

Preparation Instructions:

1. Preheat your air fryer to 180°C and spritz the air fryer basket with cooking spray.

2. Place the falafel balls in the air fryer and bake for 8-10 minutes or until golden brown and crispy.

3. While the falafel is cooking, mix together the hummus, tahini, lemon juice, salt, and pepper in a small bowl.

4. Cut the pita bread in half to create a pocket.

5. Spread the hummus mixture inside the pita bread, add the cooked falafel balls, diced tomatoes, and cucumber.

6. Place the sandwich in the air fryer and bake for 3-5 minutes or until the pita bread is warm and the falafel is heated through, flipping halfway through.

Calzone

Prep time: 10 minutes, Cook time: 10-12 minutes, Serves: 1-2

Ingredients:

1 batch of homemade or ready made pizza dough   2 tbsps. of olive oil   1 tsp. of Italian seasoning
100 g of ricotta cheese   100 g of diced pepperoni   Salt and pepper, to taste
100 g of shredded mozzarella cheese

Preparation Instructions:

1. Preheat the air fryer to 180°C.

2. Roll out the pizza dough into a large circle, about ½ cm thick.

3. In a mixing bowl, combine the ricotta cheese, pepperoni or sausage, mozzarella cheese, Italian seasoning, salt, and pepper. Mix until well combined.

4. Spread the mixture over half of the rolled out dough, leaving a 2.5 cm border around the edge.

5. Fold the other half of the dough over the filling and press the edges together to seal.

6. Brush the top of the calzone with olive oil.

7. Place the calzone in the air fryer basket and bake for 10-12 minutes or until the crust is golden brown and the filling is hot.

Chicken Fajita Wrap

Prep time: 5 minutes, Cook time: 10-12 minutes, Serves: 4

Ingredients:

cooking spray   4 tortilla wraps

200 g of sliced chicken breast

100 g of sliced peppers

100 g of sliced onions   2 tbsps. of olive oil

1 tsp. of chili powder   1 tsp. of cumin powder

Salt and pepper, to taste

Preparation Instructions:

1. Preheat your air fryer to 180°C and spritz the air fryer basket with cooking spray.

2. In a mixing bowl, combine the sliced chicken, peppers, onions, olive oil, chili powder, cumin powder, salt, and pepper. Mix until well combined.

3. Place the chicken and vegetable mixture in the air fryer basket and air fry for 8-10 minutes or until the chicken is cooked through and the vegetables are tender, flipping halfway through.

4. Remove from the air fryer and let it cool for a few minutes before serving.

5. Place the cooked chicken and vegetables in the centre of each tortilla wrap and roll them up tightly.

6. Place the wraps in the air fryer and air fry for 2-3 minutes or until the tortilla is golden brown and crispy.

Margherita Pizza

Prep time: <5 minutes, Cook time: 10 minutes, Serves: 2-4

Ingredients:

1 pre-made pizza base

100 g of crushed tomatoes

50 g of mozzarella cheese

10-15 basil leaves   1 tbsp. of olive oil

Salt and pepper, to taste

Preparation Instructions:

1. Preheat the air fryer to 180°C.

2. Place the pre-made pizza base in the air fryer basket and bake for 2-3 minutes or until it starts to puff up and become slightly crispy.

3. Remove the crust from the air fryer and spread the crushed tomatoes over the crust, leaving a small border around the edge.

4. Top with mozzarella cheese and basil leaves.

5. Drizzle with olive oil and season with salt and pepper.

6. Place the pizza back in the air fryer basket and bake for an additional 5-7 minutes or until the cheese is melted and the crust is golden brown.

7. Remove from the air fryer and let it cool for a few minutes before slicing and serving.

BBQ Pulled Pork Wrap

Prep time: <5 minutes, Cook time: 2-3 minutes, Serves: 4

Ingredients:

cooking spray   4 tortilla wraps

200 g of cooked and shredded pork

100 g of BBQ sauce   100 g of coleslaw

2 tbsps. of mayonnaise

Salt and pepper, to taste

Preparation Instructions:

1. Preheat your air fryer to 180°C and spritz the air fryer basket with cooking spray.
2. In a mixing bowl, combine the shredded pork, BBQ sauce, salt, and pepper. Mix until well combined.
3. Place the BBQ pulled pork mixture in the centre of each tortilla wrap.
4. Top with coleslaw and mayonnaise.
5. Roll the tortilla wraps tightly.
6. Place the wraps in the air fryer basket and air fry for 2-3 minutes or until the tortilla is golden brown and crispy.

Tofu Wrap

Prep time: <5 minutes, Cook time: 15 minutes, Serves: 4

Ingredients:

cooking spray   4 tortilla wraps

200 g of pressed and cubed tofu

100 g of soy sauce

100 g of diced vegetables (such as peppers, onions,

mushrooms)

2 tbsps. of sesame oil

Salt and pepper, to taste

Preparation Instructions:

1. Preheat your air fryer to 180°C and spritz the air fryer basket with cooking spray.
2. In a mixing bowl, combine the cubed tofu, soy sauce, sesame oil, salt, and pepper. Mix until well combined.
3. Place the tofu and vegetable mixture in the air fryer basket and air fry for 8-10 minutes or until the tofu is golden brown and crispy, flipping halfway through.
4. Remove from the air fryer and let it cool for a few minutes before serving.
5. Place the cooked tofu and vegetables in the centre of each tortilla wrap and roll them up tightly.
6. Place the wraps in the air fryer basket and air fry for 2-3 minutes or until the tortilla is golden brown and crispy.

CHAPTER 9: SWEET DESSERTS AND SNACKS

Peanut Butter Cookies

Prep time: <5 minutes, Cook time: 5 minutes, Serves: 20 cookies

Ingredients:

175 g sugar   230 g peanut butter   1 egg

Preparation Instructions:

1. Preheat your air fryer to 205°C and line the air fryer basket with some greaseproof paper.
2. Mix the sugar, peanut butter and egg together in a bowl.
3. Using a dessertspoon, scoop spoonfuls of the dough on the greaseproof paper.
4. Use a fork to flatten and mold in cookie shapes.
5. Place the cookies in the air fryer basket and bake for 4-5 minutes.
6. Allow time for cookies to cool before moving them off greaseproof paper.
7. After some cooling time, place cookies on a wire rack to cool.

Caramelised Banana

Prep time: <5 minutes, Cook time: 10 minutes, Serves: 2

Ingredients:

2 bananas   40 g light brown sugar   Choice of topping-whipped cream, ice cream, creme
1 tsp. cinnamon   fraiche, custard.

Preparation Instructions:

1. Mix the cinnamon and brown sugar together.
2. Preheat your air fryer to 205°C and line the air fryer basket with some greaseproof paper.
3. Peel the bananas and place them on the greaseproof paper.
4. Evenly sprinkle the cinnamon sugar mixture over the bananas.
5. Place the bananas in the air fryer basket and air fry for 8-10 minutes.
6. When the topping is caramelised and bubbling, you can remove the bananas from the air fryer.
7. Serve with your choice of topping-ice-cream, creme fraiche, custard, whipped cream etc.

Apple and Mixed Berry Crumble

Prep time: 15 minutes, Cook time: 15-20 minutes, Serves: 4

Ingredients:

Fruit Base: 300 g apples

150 g mixed berries (frozen berries will work too)

50 g brown sugar   1 tsp. cinnamon

Crumble: 200 g plain flour

100 g butter (soft)

70 g light brown sugar   50 g oats

For Serving:

cream, ice cream or custard

Preparation Instructions:

1. Preheat your air fryer to 180°C.

2. Peel apples and dice very finely.

3. Mix berries, apple slices, sugar and cinnamon together.

4. Put the berry mix into baking dish.

5. In a separate bowl, rub the flour and butter together until they have a crumbly texture.

6. Thoroughly mix the sugar and oats into this mixture.

7. Spoon the crumble over the berry and apple.

8. Place the dish in the air fryer and bake for about 15-20 minutes. The crumble topping should have a golden glow to it.

9. Serve with a choice of cream, ice cream or custard.

Scones

Prep time: 10 minutes, Cook time: 15-20 minutes, Serves: 5

Ingredients:

cooking spray   250 g self-raising flour

120 ml 7-up / sprite   120 ml whipping cream

50 g caster sugar

To glaze: Milk or egg wash

1. Preparation Instructions:

2. Preheat your air fryer to 180°C and spritz the air fryer basket with cooking spray.

3. Sieve flour in a mixing bowl.

4. Add lemonade, sugar and cream.

5. Mix together to combine ingredients. Be careful not to overmix.

6. Dredge some flour on a flat surface and knead the dough.

7. Use a scone cutter to cut individual scones.

8. Place scones in the air fryer basket with a 2 cm space between them.

9. Glaze scones with milk or egg wash and bake for 15-20 minutes.

10. Once the tops are golden, place scones on a wire cooling rack to cool.

Toffee Popcorn

Prep time: 5 minutes, Cook time: 10 minutes, Serves: 2

Ingredients:

60 g popcorn kernels   90 g butter   160 g light brown sugar

Preparation Instructions:

1. Preheat the air fryer to 200°C.
2. Put the corn kernels in the air fryer basket and air fry for about 5 minutes (or until kernels stop popping)
3. Pour popped corn kernels on a baking tray.
4. Melt the butter in microwave over a low heat.
5. Once melted, stir in brown sugar.
6. Pour mixture over popcorn.
7. Toffee popcorn is ready!

Flapjacks

Prep time: 5 minutes, Cook time: 20 minutes, Serves: 4

Ingredients:

100 g butter   100 g brown sugar   250 g porridge oats   2 tbsps. honey

Preparation Instructions:

1. Chop butter into pieces in a baking pan and put it in the air fryer to melt at 180°C for 1-2 minutes.
2. Mix the porridge oats, sugar and honey together in a separate bowl.
3. Add the oat mixture to the butter pan and mix well.
4. Bake at a reduced temperature of 160°C for 12-15 minutes.

Dried Strawberries

Prep time: <5 minutes, Cook time: 1 hour, Serves: 3

Ingredients:

200 g fresh strawberries

Preparation Instructions:

1. Preheat the air fryer to the lowest possible setting.
2. Remove stems and slice strawberries very thinly.
3. Arrange strawberry slices in air fryer basket.
4. Air fry for one hour at 90°C, turning them at the 30 minute mark.

Shortbread

Prep time: 10 minutes, additional setting time: 1-2 hours, Cook time: 8-10 minutes, Serves: 5

Ingredients:

85 g butter   30 g icing sugar   95 g plain flour

Preparation Instructions:

1. Preheat your air fryer to 170°C and line the air fryer basket with greaseproof paper.
2. Beat butter and sugar together until the two are incorporated.
3. Add flour and gently mix. Be careful not to overmix.
4. Form a ball from the dough.
5. Wrap the ball in cling film and place in the fridge for 1-2 hours.
6. When ready, take dough from the fridge and slice into 1 cm disks.
7. Place shortbread discs in the lined air fryer basket.
8. Leave plenty of space between each disk.
9. Bake for 8-10 minutes.
10. After cooling in the air fryer basket for at least 5 minutes, place biscuits on a wire cooling rack to further cool.

Chocolate Cake

Prep time: 10 minutes, Cook time: 45-50 minutes, Serves: 4

Ingredients:

70 g whipping cream   3 large eggs   30 g cocoa powder   60 ml sunflower oil
120 g caster sugar   100 g self-raising flour   40 g chopped walnuts

Preparation Instructions:

1. Preheat the air fryer to 200°C.
2. Mix the flour, eggs, sugar, cocoa powder, cream and oil in a mixing bowl.
3. Use a hand blender on a medium speed to mix the ingredients together.
4. Fold in walnuts to mix.
5. Line a cake tin with greaseproof paper.
6. Pour the batter into the lined tin.
7. Cover with tin foil and add to air fryer basket.
8. Reduce temperature to 180°C and bake for 45 minutes, until a knife comes out clean and clear from the centre of the cake.
9. Cool on a wire rack before serving.

Cinnamon Roasted Almonds

Prep time: 5 minutes, Cook time: 8 minutes, Serves: 4

Ingredients:

½ tsp. cinnamon   1 tbsp. sugar

30 g butter   130 g whole almonds

Preparation Instructions:

1. Preheat your air fryer to 200°C.
2. Melt butter in microwave or over a low heat.
3. Add almonds, sugar and cinnamon to the butter and mix well ensuring all nuts are well coated.
4. Arrange almonds in air fryer basket so none are overlapping.
5. Roast for 4 minutes.
6. After 4 minutes, stir almonds and put them back into air fryer. Roast for another 4 minutes.
7. Allow to cool before eating.

Chocolate Cheesecake

Prep time: 10 minutes, Cook time: 20 minutes, Serves: 8

Ingredients:

230 g cream cheese   45 g soft butter   2 eggs 75 g sugar   200 g melted chocolate

100 g crushed digestive biscuits   1 tsp. vanilla extract   1 tbsp. flour

Preparation Instructions:

1. Melt the butter over a low heat.
2. Once melted, add the biscuit crumbs and mix well.
3. Press the buttered biscuit crumb into the bottom of a springform tin.
4. Set in fridge / freezer while preparing the rest of the recipe.
5. In a mixing bowl, mix cream cheese and sugar.
6. Beat in eggs one at a time.
7. Add flour and vanilla extract to the filling mixture.
8. Slowly pour melted chocolate into the filling mixture.
9. Stirring all the time to evenly distribute the chocolate.
10. Spoon filling over biscuit base.
11. Preheat your air fryer to 220°C.
12. Place the springform tin in the air fryer and bake for 15-20 minutes.
13. Cool and refrigerate until cheesecake is fully set.

Air-fried Oreos

Prep time: 5 minutes, Cook time: 10 minutes, Serves: 6

Ingredients:

cooking spray   50 g plain flour

150 ml milk   1 egg

1 tsp. oil   6 oreos

Icing sugar to sprinkle

Preparation Instructions:

1. To make pancake batter, mix flour, milk, sugar and oil in a bowl.

2. Whisk until the batter is smooth.

3. Preheat your air fryer to 180°C and spritz the air fryer basket with cooking spray.

4. Dip each oreo in the pancake batter and place in air fryer basket. Keep a small gap between each oreo in the air fryer basket.

5. Air fry for 5 minutes, flip them around and then air fry for a further 2 minutes until golden.

6. Dust cooked oreos with some icing sugar.

Fairy Cakes

Prep time: 10 minutes, Cook time: 12-15 minutes, Serves: 12

Ingredients:

125 g butter, at room temperature

125 g granulated sugar 2 large eggs

125 g self-raising flour

2 tsps. baking powder   2 tbsps. milk

1 tsp. vanilla extract

Preparation Instructions:

1. Preheat your air fryer to 180°C.

2. In a large mixing bowl, cream together the butter and sugar until light and fluffy.

3. Beat in the eggs, one at a time, making sure each is fully incorporated before adding the next.

4. Sift in the flour and baking powder and fold into the mixture.

5. Stir in the milk and vanilla extract.

6. Spoon the mixture into a 12-hole fairy cake tin and place in the air fryer basket.

7. Bake for 12-15 minutes, or until golden brown and a skewer inserted into the centre of a cake comes out clean.

8. Allow to cool for a few minutes before removing from the tin and serving.

CHAPTER 10: SAVOURY SNACKS AND SIDES

Scotch Eggs

Prep time: 10 minutes, Cook time: 30 minutes, Serves: 6

Ingredients:

6 large eggs   100 g plain flour   500 g pork sausage meat

2 tsps. English mustard powder   Salt and pepper, to taste   Oil spray

Preparation Instructions:

1. Boil eggs for 6-7 minutes, then cool them in cold water. Peel the eggs and set them aside.
2. In a mixing bowl, combine the pork sausage meat, flour, mustard powder, salt, and pepper. Mix well.
3. Divide the sausage mixture into 6 equal portions and flatten each portion into a disc.
4. Place an egg in the centre of each disc and wrap the sausage mixture around the egg, making sure it is evenly coated.
5. Preheat your air fryer to 180°C.
6. Spray the scotch eggs with oil and place them in the air fryer basket.
7. Bake for 15-20 minutes or until the sausage is cooked through and golden brown.
8. Remove the scotch eggs from the air fryer and let them cool for a few minutes before serving. Enjoy!

Cauliflower Wings

Prep time: 5 minutes, Cook time: 15 minutes, Serves: 2

Ingredients:

½ head of cauliflower   30 ml olive oil   1 tsp. garlic powder   1 tsp. salt
120 ml buffalo sauce

Preparation Instructions:

1. Preheat your air fryer to 180°C.
2. Cut cauliflower into florets.
3. Stir the buffalo sauce, garlic powder and salt together.
4. Mix the cauliflower with the sauce ensuring all cauliflower is covered.
5. Grease the inside of air fryer basket with some spray oil.
6. Arrange cauliflower florets in the basket ensuring a small gap between each floret.
7. Roast for 15 minutes.
8. Remove from the air fryer and serve warm.

Crispy Green Beans

Prep time: 10 minutes, Cook time: 10 minutes, Serves: 2

Ingredients:

200 g green beans   1 egg   50 g panko bread crumbs

15 g grated parmesan cheese   ½ tsp. salt   ½ tsp. pepper

1 tsp. garlic powder   Olive oil

Preparation Instructions:

1. In a mixing bowl, combine the, breadcrumbs, parmesan, garlic powder and salt and pepper.
2. Beat the egg in a separate bowl.
3. Bread the green beans by first dipping them in the egg mix and then dredging in the breadcrumb mix.
4. Preheat your air fryer to 200°C and spray air fryer basket with olive oil.
5. Arrange the green beans in a single layer in the basket.
6. Air fry for 5-8 minutes; regularly shake the basket to turn green beans.
7. Serve when crispy!

Sausage Rolls

Prep time: 10 minutes, Cook time: 8-10 minutes, Serves: 4

Ingredients:

100 g sausage meat   1 egg   Optional: 1 tbsp. sesame seeds   Spray oil

1 sheet of prepared puff pastry

Preparation Instructions:

1. Preheat air fryer at 180°C for 10 minutes
2. Beat egg in a small bowl.
3. Spread sausage meat in the middle of a sheet of puff pastry.
4. Roll pastry around the sausage meat.
5. Using a pastry brush, brush the egg where the pastry joins.
6. Brush the length of sausage roll with egg.
7. Sprinkle with sesame seeds if using.
8. Cut the stuffed pastry sheet into lengths of 4 cm.
9. Close each end of sausage rolls.
10. Spray air fryer basket with oil.
11. Place the sausage rolls in the air fryer basket.
12. Bake for 8-10 minutes until the pastry is golden.

Crunchy Corn

Prep time: 5 minutes, Cook time: 7 minutes, Serves: 2

Ingredients:

2 ears of corn ½ tsp. salt ½ tsp. pepper 30 g butter

Preparation Instructions:

1. Melt butter in the microwave or over a low heat.
2. Preheat air fryer to 200°C.
3. Toss the corn in the butter.
4. Season with salt and pepper.
5. Place the corn in the air fryer basket and air fry for 5 minutes.
6. Turn and air fry for a further 2 minutes.
7. Serve warm.

Pita Bread Chips

Prep time: <5 minutes, Cook time: 8 minutes, Serves: 4

Ingredients:

4 pita bread pockets 2 tbsps. olive oil 1½ tsps. rosemary 2 tsps. sea salt / rock salt

Preparation Instructions:

1. Preheat your air fryer to 160°C.
2. Cut pita bread into triangles.
3. Mix oil, rosemary and sea salt in a small bowl.
4. Drizzle oil and herbs over pita breads.
5. Air fry for 4 minutes.
6. Toss pita chips and air fry for a further 4 minutes.

Spiced Sweet Potatoes

Prep time: 10 minutes, Cook time: 15 minutes, Serves: 4

Ingredients:

2 large sweet potatoes Olive oil 1 tsp. paprika 1 tsp. cumin
1 tsp. onion powder 1 tsp. salt 1 tsp. black pepper

Preparation Instructions:

1. Chop the sweet potatoes into small cubes of about 2 cm.
2. Combine all the spices and seasonings in a bowl and mix.
3. Add the sweet potatoes and a drizzle of olive oil to the seasoning mix.
4. Stir well and ensure sweet potatoes are covered with spices.
5. Preheat your air fryer to 200°C and spray air fryer basket with some oil.
6. Add the sweet potato mix to the basket and bake for 15 minutes. Shake the basket and spray more oil often to ensure crisp and even sweet potatoes.

Halloumi Fries

Prep time: 5 minutes, Cook time: 10 minutes, Serves: 4

Ingredients:

35 g plain flour   1 tsp. garlic powder   235 g halloumi cheese   Spray oil
Sprinkle of salt and pepper   Optional: 1 tsp. smoked paprika

Preparation Instructions:

1. Slice halloumi in 1-2 cm sticks.
2. Combine garlic, flour, salt and pepper in a bowl.
3. Preheat air fryer to 200°C and spray the air fryer basket with spray oil.
4. Dredge the halloumi in the flour mixture.
5. Arrange halloumi in a single layer in air fryer basket.
6. Air fry for 6-10 minutes, until fries are golden.

Air Fryer Olives

Prep time: 5 minutes, Cook time: 10-12 minutes, Serves: 2

Ingredients:

cooking spray   20 g plain flour   15 g grated parmesan cheese   120 g olives
30 g panko bread crumbs   1 egg

Preparation Instructions:

1. Preheat your air fryer to 200°C and spritz the air fryer basket with cooking spray.
2. Mix parmesan and bread crumbs together.
3. Prepare a coating station with three bowls-egg in one bowl, flour in another and parmesan bread crumbs in the third bowl.
4. Bread olives by placing them in flour first,then egg and finally breadcrumbs.
5. Put the breaded olives in the air fryer basket.
6. Air fry for 10-12 minutes.

Parmesan Potatoes

Prep time: 5 minutes, Cook time: 25 minutes, Serves: 4

Ingredients:

400 g potatoes 2 tbsps. olive oil   40 g grated parmesan
1 tsp. salt   ½ black pepper

Preparation Instructions:

1. Peel and dice potatoes.
2. In a mixing bowl, mix salt, pepper, parmesan and oil.
3. Add the potatoes to the mixture.
4. Preheat the air fryer at 200°C for 2 minutes.
5. Place potatoes to the air fryer basket and air fry for 15 minutes, shaking basket to toss potatoes.
6. Air fry for another 10 minutes.
7. Serve and enjoy!

Prosciutto Wrapped Asparagus

Prep time: <5 minutes, Cook time: 5 minutes, Serves: 2

Ingredients:

300 g asparagus   8 slices prosciutto

Preparation Instructions:

1. Preheat your air fryer to 180°C.
2. Trim asparagus by removing the ends.
3. Wrap each asparagus spear with a slice of prosciutto.
4. Place in the air fryer basket and air fry for 5 minutes.

Garlic Bread

Prep time: <5 minutes, Cook time: 5 minutes, Serves: 5

Ingredients:

cooking spray   5 tbsps. butter   50 g parmesan cheese
3 tbsps. garlic (minced)   French Baguette   1 tbsp. parsley

Preparation Instructions:

1. Preheat your air fryer to 175°C and spritz the air fryer basket with cooking spray.
2. Soften butter and mix well with garlic, parsley and parmesan cheese.
3. Slice French baguette and spread garlic butter on each slice.
4. Put the bread in the air fryer basket.
5. Air fry for 5 minutes.

Crispy Chickpeas

Prep time: 5 minutes, Cook time: 15 minutes, Serves: 2

Ingredients:

250 g chickpeas   ½ tsp. garlic powder
½ tsp. smoked paprika
¼ tsp. black pepper   1 tbsp. olive oil

Preparation Instructions:

1. Drain chickpeas and dry them completely. Moisture will prevent the chickpeas from becoming crispy.
2. Put dried chickpeas in an air fryer basket and roast for 12-15 minutes at a low heat-90°C.
3. In a mixing bowl, combine spices and olive oil.
4. Mix chickpeas thoroughly with oil and spices.

APPENDIX 1: 365 DAY MEAL PLAN

Day 1-5	Fish Fillets	Buttermilk Chicken	Air Fryer Baked Butternut Squash	Porridge Bread	Cinnamon Roasted Almonds
Day 6-10	Kung Pao Chicken	Apple and Mixed Berry Crumble	French Toast	Zesty Parmesan Asparagus	Maple Mustard Salmon
Day 11-15	Breakfast Energy Balls	Crispy Chicken Tenders	Tuna Melt	Pork and Apple Skewers	Fairy Cakes
Day 16-20	BBQ Chicken Sandwich	Air-fried Prawns	Cauliflower Steaks	Dried Strawberries	Breakfast Quinoa
Day 21-25	Banana Bread	Asian Style Tofu Kebabs	Shortbread	Scallops	Sweet Potato Fries
Day 26-30	Korean Style Beef	Crispy Chickpeas	Breakfast Cookies	Vegetable Kebabs	Roasted Peppers
Day 31-35	Maple Glazed Turkey	Roasted Cauliflower	Toffee Popcorn	Blueberry Muffins	Crab Cakes
Day 36-40	Chocolate Cheesecake	Omelette	French Dip Sandwich	Asian Style Pork	Tandoori Chicken
Day 41-45	Duck Breast	Falafel Sandwich	Tofu Scramble	Pita Bread Chips	Air Fryer Mackerel
Day 40-50	Lamb Koftas	Tofu	Air Fryer Olives	Greek Wrap	Granola
Day 51-55	Fish and Chips	Cauliflower Wings	Lemon Herbed Chicken	Pakoras	BBQ Chicken Pizza
Day 56-60	Spiced Sweet Potatoes	Lemon Garlic Salmon	Peanut Butter Cookies	Breakfast Burrito	Garlic Bread
Day 61-65	Citrus and Herb Turkey Breast	Tofu Wrap	Egg Cups	Flapjacks	Lemon Pepper Cod
Day 66-70	Margherita Pizza	Pork Chops	Cauliflower Buffalo Wings	Parmesan Potatoes	Quesadillas

Day 71-75	Sweet Potato Hash Browns	Halloumi Fries	Cajun Cod	Orange Glazed Duck	Calzone
Day 76-80	Air-fried Oreos	Aubergine Fries	Air-fried Scampi	Caramelised Banana	Meatballs
Day 81-85	Crispy Green Beans	Fish Fingers	Veggie Sandwich	Air Fryer Baked Oats	Scones
Day 86-90	Portobello Mushrooms	Sausage Rolls	Stuffed Peppers	Air Fryer Roasted Beetroot	Chicken Kiev
Day 91-95	Breakfast Potatoes	Air Fryer Roasted Vegetables	Garlic Parmesan Brussels Sprouts	Spicy Turkey	Chocolate Cake
Day 96-100	Chickpea and Sweet Potato Fritters	Teriyaki Salmon	Air Fryer Baked Courgette	Caramelised Banana	Burgers
Day 101-105	BBQ Pulled Pork Wrap	BBQ Ribs	Crispy Kale	Duck Leg	Crunchy Corn
Day 106-110	Lamb Kebabs	Prosciutto Wrapped Asparagus	Parmesan Crusted Chicken	Air Fryer Baked Butternut Squash	Fish Pie
Day 111-115	Scotch Eggs	Five Spiced Duck	Cuban Sandwich	Macaroni and Cheese Bites	Calamari
Day 116-120	BBQ Turkey Breast	Chicken Fajita Wrap	Mussels	Apple and Mixed Berry Crumble	Falafel
Day 121-125	Garlic Bread	Quinoa Stuffed Peppers	BBQ Chicken Sandwich	Tofu	Veggie Fried Rice
Day 126-130	Tofu Scramble	Buttermilk Chicken	Roasted Peppers	Maple Mustard Salmon	Air Fryer Olives
Day 131-135	Kung Pao Chicken	Pita Bread Chips	Cauliflower Steaks	Zesty Parmesan Asparagus	Lamb Kebabs
Day 136-140	Greek Wrap	Fish Fingers	Asian Style Tofu Kebabs	Omelette	Crispy Chickpeas
Day 141-145	Toffee Popcorn	Duck Breast	Porridge Bread	Falafel Sandwich	Air-fried Scampi

Day 146-150	Pork Chops	Orange Glazed Duck	Dried Strawberries	Lemon Pepper Cod	French Dip Sandwich
Day 151-155	Tandoori Chicken	Aubergine Fries	Quesadillas	Scones	Lamb Koftas
Day 156-160	Fairy Cakes	French Toast	Tuna Melt	Fish Fillets	Granola
Day 161-165	Pork and Apple Skewers	Spiced Sweet Potatoes	Maple Glazed Turkey	Air Fryer Baked Oats	Tofu Wrap
Day 166-170	Fish and Chips	Cauliflower Buffalo Wings	Shortbread	Crispy Chicken Tenders	Sweet Potato Fries
Day 171-175	Cinnamon Roasted Almonds	Garlic Parmesan Brussels Sprouts	Breakfast Energy Balls	Crab Cakes	Pakoras
Day 176-180	Calamari	Stuffed Peppers	Prosciutto Wrapped Asparagus	Portobello Mushrooms	Maple Glazed Turkey
Day 181-185	Flapjacks	Vegetable Kebabs	Roasted Cauliflower	Banana Bread	Scallops
Day 186-190	Blueberry Muffins	BBQ Chicken Pizza	Crispy Green Beans	Cajun Cod	Chickpea and Sweet Potato Fritters
Day 191-195	Asian Style Pork	Scotch Eggs	Citrus and Herb Turkey Breast	Cuban Sandwich	Sweet Potato Hash Browns
Day 196-200	BBQ Pulled Pork Wrap	Breakfast Cookies	Spicy Turkey	Teriyaki Salmon	Air-fried Oreos
Day 201-205	Air Fryer Roasted Vegetables	Five Spiced Duck	Egg Cups	Chocolate Cake	Air Fryer Mackerel
Day 206-210	Breakfast Burrito	Halloumi Fries	Chicken Fajita Wrap	Macaroni and Cheese Bites	Parmesan Crusted Chicken
Day 211-215	Chickpea and Sweet Potato Fritters	Air Fryer Baked Courgette	Air-fried Prawns	Chocolate Cheesecake	Burgers
Day 216-220	Mussels	Crispy Kale	Duck Leg	BBQ Ribs	Crunchy Corn

Day 221-225	Parmesan Potatoes	Lemon Garlic Salmon	French Dip Sandwich	Breakfast Quinoa	Peanut Butter Cookies
Day 226-230	Breakfast Potatoes	Sausage Rolls	Cauliflower Buffalo Wings	Calzone	Lemon Herbed Chicken
Day 231-235	Quinoa Stuffed Peppers	Margherita Pizza	Korean Style Beef	Chicken Kiev	Cauliflower Wings
Day 236-240	Air-fried Scampi	Meatballs	Veggie Fried Rice	Veggie Sandwich	BBQ Turkey Breast
Day 241-245	Orange Glazed Duck	Air Fryer Olives	Roasted Cauliflower	Fish Pie	Flapjacks
Day 246-250	Caramelised Banana	Fish Fingers	Prosciutto Wrapped Asparagus	Buttermilk Chicken	Asian Style Pork
Day 251-255	Cauliflower Steaks	Apple and Mixed Berry Crumble	Air Fryer Baked Butternut Squash	Scallops	Kung Pao Chicken
Day 256-260	Garlic Bread	Tandoori Chicken	Stuffed Peppers	Roasted Peppers	Falafel
Day 261-265	BBQ Ribs	Scones	Asian Style Tofu Kebabs	Sweet Potato Fries	Calamari
Day 266-270	Air Fryer Roasted Beetroot	Air Fryer Mackerel	BBQ Chicken Sandwich	Cinnamon Roasted Almonds	Quesadillas
Day 271-275	Fish Fillets	Fairy Cakes	Tofu Scramble	Greek Wrap	Shortbread
Day 276-280	Pita Bread Chips	Burgers	BBQ Chicken Pizza	Crab Cakes	Tofu Wrap
Day 281-285	Pork and Apple Skewers	BBQ Pulled Pork Wrap	Portobello Mushrooms	Toffee Popcorn	Breakfast Cookies
Day 286-290	Breakfast Potatoes	Tuna Melt	Duck Breast	Maple Mustard Salmon	Crispy Chicken Tenders
Day 291-295	Margherita Pizza	Mussels	Pakoras	Sausage Rolls	Pork Chops
Day 296-300	Crispy Chickpeas	French Toast	Calzone	Spicy Turkey	Scotch Eggs

Day 301-305	Macaroni and Cheese Bites	Crunchy Corn	Tofu	Sweet Potato Hash Browns	Zesty Parmesan Asparagus
Day 306-310	Prosciutto Wrapped Asparagus	Duck Leg	Meatballs	Chicken Fajita Wrap	Cajun Cod
Day 311-315	Crispy Chicken Tenders	Halloumi Fries	Quinoa Stuffed Peppers	Air Fryer Baked Courgette	Blueberry Muffins
Day 316-320	Porridge Bread	Maple Glazed Turkey	Falafel Sandwich	Korean Style Beef	Dried Strawberries
Day 321-325	Teriyaki Salmon	Cauliflower Wings	Breakfast Energy Balls	Cuban Sandwich	BBQ Turkey Breast
Day 326-330	Chickpea and Sweet Potato Fritters	Veggie Fried Rice	Air-fried Prawns	Granola	Spiced Sweet Potatoes
Day 331-335	Chocolate Cake	Fish and Chips	Air Fryer Roasted Beetroot	Lemon Herbed Chicken	Falafel
Day 336-340	Chicken Kiev	Crispy Kale	Lemon Garlic Salmon	Crispy Green Beans	Omelette
Day 341-345	Egg Cups	Parmesan Crusted Chicken	Aubergine Fries	Lamb Koftas	Peanut Butter Cookies
Day 346-350	Flapjacks	Breakfast Burrito	Garlic Parmesan Brussels Sprouts	Lemon Pepper Cod	Vegetable Kebabs
Day 351-355	Five Spiced Duck	Air-fried Oreos	Lamb Kebabs	French Dip Sandwich	Banana Bread
Day 356-360	Air-fried Scampi	Citrus and Herb Turkey Breast	Air Fryer Roasted Vegetables	Breakfast Quinoa	Parmesan Potatoes
Day 361-365	Veggie Sandwich	Cauliflower Buffalo Wings	Air Fryer Baked Oats	Chocolate Cheesecake	Fish Pie

APPENDIX 2: RECIPES INDEX

Printed in Great Britain
by Amazon

19933007R00045